"To read these profound theological meditation﹐
fourth-century monk, Evagrius Ponticus: 'the bosom of the Lord is
knowledge of God; the one who rests there will be a theologian.' Robert
Imbelli is, by Evagrius' standard, a master theologian. He offers evocative
explorations of such diverse sources as the documents of Vatican II, the
theology of Pope Benedict XVI, Dante, iconography, hymns, and the
writings of Simone Weil and Etty Hillesum. In these pages we reap the fruit
of a long career of theological scholarship and biblically informed preaching.
Under Imbelli's tutelage we experience the rewarding cultivation of a
'Christic imagination' too often neglected in contemporary theology."

> —Richard R. Gaillardetz
> Joseph McCarthy Professor of Catholic Systematic Theology
> Boston College

"By careful scriptural exegesis Robert Imbelli properly places Christ at the
center of our Christian faith and lives, governing the identity, mission, and
worship of the church. All this is illustrated from Christian poetry and art
over the centuries in such a way as to encourage and inspire in a freshly
imagined way the new evangelization that the Second Vatican Council saw
to be sorely needed in our time and world. *Rekindling the Christic
Imagination* could serve in a classic way the theological education of
candidates for the priesthood as well as refreshing those already in the
ministry (including Protestants!)."

> —Dr. Geoffrey Wainwright
> Robert Earl Cushman Professor Emeritus of Christian Theology
> Duke Divinity School

"Robert Imbelli's beautifully written book on the centrality of Christ for the
Catholic faith does fair justice both to trinitarian theology and to the
mystery of the church in the light of Christ. It should be read in the manner
it was written: in a spirit of contemplative reflection. The author's intention
of being a work of *aggiornamento* and *ressourcement* is fully realized."

> —Lawrence S. Cunningham
> John A. O'Brien Professor of Theology (Emeritus)
> The University of Notre Dame

"This is a beautiful, profound, and precise book. Theology, for Imbelli, is a matter of meditative, Christ-centered reasoning, and he shows what this means by responding to Christ as imaged by and present in four works of visual art. This way of working gives to Imbelli's prose and pattern of thought a limpidity through which the face of Jesus can be seen in chiaroscuro. It also makes possible a depth of theological thinking that undercuts and reconciles the tired divisions in the American church. I read Imbelli's book immediately after reading Pope Francis' *Evangelii Gaudium*, and what Imbelli does exemplifies what Francis recommends: a recovery of the joy of thinking about and approaching Jesus that transcends internal oppositions and permits *ressourcement* and *aggiornamento* to kiss. Imbelli's work is theological mystagogy of a very high order."

> —Paul J. Griffiths
> Warren Chair of Catholic Theology
> Duke Divinity School

"Imbelli doesn't just talk about mystagogy; he practices it. Drawing on poets and painters, *Rekindling the Christic Imagination* aims for the reader to be 'possessed' by Christ. Imbelli rightly refuses to choose between *aggiornamento* and *ressourcement*, recognizing that their unity is found in a renewed focus on Jesus Christ himself as the center of our theological endeavors. The result is a biblically grounded and theologically rich meditation on Christological, trinitarian, eucharistic, and ecclesial themes."

> —Hans Boersma
> J. I. Packer Professor of Theology
> Regent College
> Vancouver, British Columbia, Canada

"Painters and poets help Imbelli distill decades of preaching and teaching into a fine evangelical wine. Charles Taylor's call to recover a sense of what the incarnation can mean inspires an accessible and moving account of church, eucharist, and Vatican II as Christic calls to holiness in the world. A meditative gem of a book!"

> —William L. Portier
> Mary Ann Spearin Chair of Catholic Theology
> University of Dayton

"I had the good fortune of reading Fr. Imbelli's book right before Christmas. The small but rich book proved to be a most rewarding meditation on the surpassing mystery of the incarnation—theologically fecund, spiritually edifying, and aesthetically appealing. The content, style, and artistic appeal of the book gives tangible witness to the fact that truth, goodness, and beauty are united in the person of the crucified and risen Christ. Fr. Imbelli's very accessibly written 'mystagogy' is a compelling invitation into the mystery of Christ and an important contribution to the New Evangelization."

—Reinhard Hütter
Professor of Christian Theology
Duke University Divinity School

"Here is clear and beautiful writing at a peaceful pace and tone. With quiet confidence Robert Imbelli places the concept of revelation, especially in its fresh articulation in Vatican II's *Dei Verbum*, at the center of the theological enterprise. And as the center of revelation he places with renewed clarity the figure of Jesus Christ. This is a model of how to advance theological thinking in the coming years. Faith, wonder, and adoration accompany sharp critical thought in exposing the uniqueness of the treasure given us by God in Jesus Christ."

—Jeremy Driscoll, OSB
Pontifical Athenaeum Sant' Anselmo,
Rome/Mount Angel Seminary

"Robert Imbelli's new book uses art and literature to show how the new evangelization needs to be rooted in the paschal mystery of Christ and Vatican II's universal call to holiness. Fresh and original in its approach and profoundly incarnational, this timely book is a rich resource for adult education and introductory courses in theology."

—Thomas P. Rausch, SJ
T. Marie Chilton Professor of Catholic Theology
Loyola Marymount University
Los Angeles, California

"Drawing on sources artistic, literary, spiritual, and theological, Robert Imbelli provides a splendid and intellectually stimulating exploration of the New Evangelization. Anyone interested in preaching, teaching, or pastoral work should read this uplifting book."

—Very Reverend Robert Barron
Rector / President, University of Saint Mary of the Lake /
Mundelein Seminary
Mundelein, Illinois

Rekindling the Christic Imagination

Theological Meditations for the New Evangelization

Robert P. Imbelli

LITURGICAL PRESS
Collegeville, Minnesota

www.litpress.org

2	3	4	5	6	7	8	9

Library of Congress Control Number: 2013955286

ISBN 978-0-8146-3550-6
ISBN 978-0-8146-3575-9 (ebook)

In loving memory of my mother, Julia Piro Imbelli

Tu se' lo mio maestro e 'l mio autore

—Dante

Contents

We do not proclaim ourselves, but Jesus Christ as Lord—ourselves your servants for Jesus' sake. For God, who said, "Let light shine out of darkness," has shone in our hearts, giving the light of the knowledge of the glory of God on the face of Christ.

—2 Corinthians 4:5-6

When Christ comes, we enjoy a spiritual Spring: for in Christ we bloom again to newness of life, and human nature is fulfilled as it comes to flower and to bear fruit.

—Saint Cyril of Alexandria

The Spirit and the Bride say, "Come!" . . . Amen. Come, Lord Jesus!

—Revelation 22:17, 20

Preface

In his apostolic letter *Novo Millennio Ineunte*, Pope John Paul II marked the Great Jubilee of the Year 2000 and concluded: "Now that the Jubilee has ended I feel more than ever in duty bound to point to the council as *the great grace bestowed on the Church in the twentieth century*: there we find a sure compass by which to take our bearings in the century now beginning."[1]

It has proved so for me. I had the wonderful privilege of studying in Rome during the four sessions of the Second Vatican Council. I experienced firsthand the intellectual excitement and spiritual energy of those years. The council and its magnificent documents have indeed provided "a sure compass" in my almost fifty years of priestly and theological ministry.

The council, as is well known, undertook its labors under the standards of *ressourcement* and *aggiornamento*. *Ressourcement* indicated the council's effort to rediscover, with fresh eyes, the wellsprings of the faith, in particular the Scriptures themselves and the reception of and reflection upon the Scriptures by the early bishops and theologians of the church. In doing so, the council recovered a broader and deeper sense of tradition than had characterized Catholic understanding prior to the council.[2]

By *aggiornamento*, the council indicated its intention to bring the Good News of Jesus Christ proclaimed by the tradition into the world of today, addressing the aspirations and concerns of contemporary men and women in language that speaks to them in a way both intelligible and pastorally inviting.

The council itself was able to hold these two movements of rediscovery and renewal in creative tension, channeling the centrifugal forces that could pull them apart. Concretely, bishops and theologians collaborated in composing the documents, enabling diverse voices to unite in contrapuntal harmony. This achievement was due in no small measure to the patient oversight and wise leadership of two bishops of Rome, Pope John XXIII and Pope Paul VI.

The "event" of the council cannot be restricted merely to its texts, the sixteen documents the council produced and promulgated; nor even to those exciting years, from October, 1962 to December, 1965, when the council was in session. It includes both these, of course; but it also comprises the years since, years in which the teachings and initiatives of the council were received and implemented. This "reception" of the council continues today. Hence the event of the council is continuing today.[3]

Most certainly, the texts have a privileged place in the ongoing interpretation of the council. They are the continuing point of reference and guide in our ever-new pastoral and theological labors. They constitute our compass. But compasses must be read, and they can be read accurately or inaccurately. Texts must be interpreted, and they can be interpreted selectively or comprehensively. Hence the challenge we face.

The challenge is to appropriate the texts of the council in a comprehensive way that does justice to all of the documents it bequeathed the church.[4] Nonetheless, not all the documents of the council are of equal weight. The council itself signaled its intent by designating four of its documents as "constitutions," hence as of primary importance: These are, of course, *Sacrosanctum Concilium* (The Constitution on the Sacred Liturgy), *Lumen Gentium* (The Dogmatic Constitution on the Church), *Gaudium et Spes* (The Pastoral Constitution on the Church in the Modern World), and *Dei Verbum* (The Dogmatic Constitution on Divine Revelation). If these represent the interpretive keys to the council's intentions, they must not be read in isolated fashion, but "intertextually," tracing their interconnections and discerning the fundamental principles that guide the council's vision.

Among the four, I maintain that *Dei Verbum* deserves to be considered a "first among equals." The reason is simple. Unless God has revealed himself fully through Jesus Christ in the Holy Spirit, then the church is without foundation and the liturgy a merely human construct. *Dei Verbum* makes this foundational claim: "By this revelation the deepest truth, both about God and about human salvation, shines forth for us in Christ, who is himself both the mediator and the fullness of all revelation" (2).[5]

Postconciliar Crisis and Challenge

In the years following the council, the creative tension it embodied has often slackened. Without the complement of *aggiornamento*, *ressourcement* risks becoming mere antiquarianism: a museum tour through ancient artifacts. Without *ressourcement*, *aggiornamento* can easily slip into a cultural accommodation that lacks substance: salt losing its savor. Without fruitful dialogue and faith-filled exchange, bishops and theologians risk becoming partisans of causes, viewing each other with suspicion.[6] The postconciliar years have, unhappily, all too often witnessed such division.

Partial and partisan readings of the council and its documents account for some of the fragmentation and polarization we have experienced. But I suggest that these are symptoms of a more severe crisis: an eclipse of the enlivening and unifying center of the faith. That center is Jesus Christ himself, crucified under Pontius Pilate, risen and present as Lord and head of his body, the church. Absent this concrete and vivifying center, fragmentation and division ensue.

At first blush, this claim may appear overstated. Do not Catholics affirm the absolute centrality of Jesus Christ at every liturgy, making their every prayer "through Jesus Christ our Lord"? Indeed they do. Yet there remains the sad and intractable fact that attendance at liturgy on the part of Catholics has precipitously declined since the council. Moreover, in some theological circles, an odd aversion to affirmations of the uniqueness and universality of Jesus Christ has taken hold.[7] One manifestation of this is the relative neglect of the "Constitution on Divine Revelation" since the council—as though its robust confession of the revelatory primacy of Jesus Christ is "too hard a word," echoing the disciples who turn away from Jesus in John's gospel (John 6:60).

I am not alone in offering this diagnosis of our present plight. In a remarkable *cri du coeur*, Benedict XVI spoke of what impelled him to write his books on Jesus of Nazareth. He wrote: "[faith's] point of reference is being placed in doubt: Intimate friendship with Jesus, on which everything depends, is in danger of clutching at thin air."[8] Benedict is referring here to certain trends in biblical scholarship that either disclaim any solid knowledge of Jesus or reduce him to a prophetic figure in the history of Israel. Such academic ruminations invariably infiltrate via the media to wider audiences.

Lest the assertion appear to be special pleading, a prominent Catholic New Testament scholar seconds Benedict's alarm. Luke Timothy Johnson laments that "the truth of the Gospel concerning Jesus the Lord has been eroded over a period of centuries, not through direct attack by Christianity's cultured despisers, but through a steady process of revision by theologians who seem either unaware of or not to care about the consequences of their capitulation to the premises of Christianity's cultured despisers." Nor does Johnson spare bishops their share of responsibility for the "Christological collapse" that he discerns. He decries their "failure adequately to address the erosion of the heart of the Gospel."[9]

As a final witness to this loss of cogent and compelling Christocentricity, I cite the late Cardinal Avery Dulles. In the last book he prepared for publication, literally as he lay dying, Cardinal Dulles wrote of tendencies in contemporary Catholic theology "that inhibit a vigorous program of evangelization." Foremost among them is what he calls "soteriological pluralism": the tendency among some theologians "to deny that Jesus Christ is the Savior of the world." In the name of "openness" and "tolerance," they hold that each religion has its own way of salvation. Jesus may be the savior for Christians, but this confession need not preclude acknowledgement of other savior figures.[10] Such a view clearly compromises the Christic center of faith taught by the council. It provides no basis or motivation for a new evangelization.

My conviction is that the way forward to a comprehensive reception of the council lies in the direction that *Dei Verbum* has affirmed: the way that recognizes in Jesus, crucified and risen, the Word of God in person. *Dei Verbum* confesses that "Jesus completes the work of revelation . . . above all by his death and his glorious resurrection from the dead, and his sending of the Spirit of Truth." Revelation, in sum, is the joyful realization that in Christ "God is with us, to free us from the darkness of sin and death, and to raise us up to eternal life" (4).

Such insistence on the centrality of Christ by no means detracts from the trinitarian content of the faith. The documents of Vatican II, *Dei Verbum* and *Lumen Gentium* in particular, testify to this. They are explicitly Christocentric and also replete with trinitarian confession and affirmation. How could it be otherwise, since the church proclaims Jesus to be the eternal Son of the Father?

Indeed, the sole theological basis for confessing the triune God is the claim the Apostolic Tradition makes regarding the uniqueness of Jesus. Trinitarian theology is the necessary fruit of professing the divinity of Jesus. Further, the Holy Spirit, whom the Father sends, is not some anonymous, faceless force, but the Spirit of the Son mirrored in a multitude who pray in Jesus' name. The Letter to the Galatians, written in the mid-first century, already proclaims the lived trinitarian faith: "God has sent the Spirit of his Son into our hearts, crying, 'Abba, Father'!" (Gal 4:6).[11]

Nor does a Christocentric approach to theology entail "Christomonism" (as some seem to fear)—the supposed exclusive emphasis on Jesus. For, as we have seen, one cannot do justice to Jesus short of seeing him within a fully trinitarian frame of reference. Moreover, as "the firstborn of the dead" (Col 1:18), Jesus is "the firstborn of many brothers and sisters" (Rom 8:29). Jesus Christ is, indeed, the Center, but the eschatological goal is the "recapitulation of all in Christ" (Eph 1:10). This eschatological goal inspires and sustains the prayer and action of believers.[12] Thus the very heart of the pastoral-theological ministry of Saint Augustine is to foster the growth of the *totus Christus*, the whole Christ, Head and members, enlivened by the Holy Spirit.

The proper work of the Holy Spirit is to bring about the incorporation of men and women into Christ, thereby constituting the one body of redeemed humanity. Hence, in contrast to those who would separate Christ and the Spirit, I fully endorse Yves Congar's axiom: "If I were to draw one conclusion from the whole of my work on the Holy Spirit, I would express it in these words: no Christology without pneumatology and no pneumatology without Christology."[13]

The Present Work

The present book, with its introduction and four sections, seeks to meditate upon this Christic Center[14] of Catholic faith as it expands from its Center in Christ into the intimately interrelated realities of Eucharist, church, and, ultimately, Trinity. Karl Rahner has taught us to see synoptically: we contemplate not many discrete mysteries but the inexhaustible Mystery of the God who is love, revealing and saving by the outpouring of his love upon the world through the inseparable missions of Christ and the Spirit. The book thus hopes to offer in a unitary vision the distinctive content of Christian faith: the Glory of God on the face of Christ Jesus.

The presentation aims to be more meditative than discursive. Indeed, it aspires to offer a "mystagogical" meditation: one that evokes the Mystery to which it inadequately points.[15] Thus the four works of art that accompany the sections are integral to the book's purpose. It hopes thereby to further the project, heralded by Hans Urs von Balthasar, of restoring the aesthetic to full citizenship in the theological enterprise. In addition, it seeks to foster another of von Balthasar's goals: a "praying theology"—one that arises from and leads to prayer.

Finally, the book aspires to be a modest contribution to the "New Evangelization" to which all the popes since the council have summoned the church. This evangelization is, at its heart, the call to renewed conversion to Jesus Christ and the passionate desire to share his Good News with others that they "may have life and have it to the full" (John 10:10). As Pope John Paul II wrote: "We are certainly not seduced by the naïve expectation that, faced with the great challenges of our time, we shall find some magic formula. No, we shall not be saved by a formula but by a Person, and the assurance which he gives us: *I am with you!*"[16]

I conclude this preface with words of gratitude for those whose friendship and companionship have sustained me during these postconciliar years and nourished my faith.

I remember gratefully my brother Michael and my sister-in-law Lillian; also the Reverend John J. Connelly and the people of

Sacred Heart Parish, Newton Centre; the Reverend Robert Grippo and the people of Saint Theresa Parish, the Bronx; the Reverend William P. Leahy, SJ, president of Boston College and the Church in the Twenty-First Century Initiative he founded; and my colleagues at Boston College: Professors Khaled Anatolios and Boyd Taylor Coolman.

Five friends deserve special mention for their insight and inspiration, both theological and aesthetic, over the years: Professors Christopher Ruddy and Mark Burrows, the Reverend Richard Smith, the Reverend James Massa, and Timothy Schilling.

My archbishop, Cardinal Timothy Dolan, has my thanks for his gracious encouragement, as does Joseph Lynaugh, for the spur of his Aristotelian common sense.

Twenty-seven years of teaching both graduate and undergraduate students at Boston College have, in turn, taught me so much. A few names to represent the many: Anthony and AnneMarie Coleman, Christopher Collins, SJ, Peter Fritz, Brother Isaiah Hoffman, CFR, Andrew Meszaros, Nathaniel Peters, Christopher Rakovec, Andrew Salzmann, Michael Sickler, Shane Ulbrich, Robert Van Alstyne, SJ, and Robert Withers. Special thanks are due Nathaniel Peters for his assistance in obtaining the images and compiling the indexes.

Finally, I am thankful to those theologians who have most influenced my own journey: the late Cardinal Avery Dulles, SJ, the late Frans Jozef van Beeck, SJ, and Pope Emeritus Benedict XVI.

I joyfully join Saint Paul in prayer: "I thank my God in all my remembrance of you. . . . I am sure that he who began a good work in you will bring it to completion at the day of Christ Jesus" (Phil 1:3, 6).

August 15, 2013
Solemnity of the Assumption of Our Lady

Introduction

Charles Taylor and Pope Benedict XVI: Faith Today

In a now famous prophecy, uttered shortly after the close of Vatican II, Karl Rahner predicted: "the devout Christian of the future will either be a 'mystic,' one who has 'experienced' something, or he will cease to be anything at all."[1] Rahner's intuition has been amply verified. The growing secularization of Western culture and society, and its increasing spread beyond the North Atlantic region, excludes God from its "social imaginary," to borrow a phrase from the Canadian Catholic philosopher, Charles Taylor,[2] and seeks aggressively to restrict religion to a private sphere that has minimal relevance to the public square.

By the "social imaginary" Taylor does not intend, in the first instance, theories or even ideas. He focuses first on the images and stories that enkindle our imaginations and shape our sensibilities, the common understandings and practices that make beliefs plausible. Just as five hundred years ago the social imaginary was permeated with a sense of the reality and providence of God, today belief in God is only one of the many options our contemporaries have. Believers, of course, are by no means exempt from this ambient culture. At least in the Western world we have, for the most part, lost the sustaining environments of neighborhood and community that made belief seem normal and natural. The air around us, to use the title of Taylor's book, is very much that of "a secular age." Thus the relevance of Rahner's affirmation.

Taylor goes on at great length to characterize features of contemporary secularity. He applauds many of its achievements: its celebration of individual rights, its espousal of racial and religious tolerance, and its respect for freedom of conscience. All these are gains, some of them acquired in the face of stubborn ecclesiastical resistance. All the more credible, then, are Taylor's critiques of secularity's blind spots, even its dark side. Among these is its rampant individualism: its promotion of the "buffered" self, allergic to relational entanglements and commitments. A further symptom of secularity's malaise is its apparent rejection of any transcendent reference, its practical atheism that risks confining humanity in a one-dimensional world. Very often a frantic consumerism strives to fill the void left by this absence of an enlivening transcendence. Its mantra seem to be: "I buy, therefore I am."

For Taylor, however (and this is striking), the philosophical and scientific developments that have spawned the modern age and the social imaginary to which it gives rise do not, of themselves, necessarily terminate in unbelief. They may also support a renewed belief.[3] Though belief can no longer be taken for granted, neither can it be ruled out of court. What counts is the believer's appropriation of his or her faith within a community that does not retreat into a cultural ghetto, but engages modernity with appreciative and critical discernment. Thus Taylor is very much an advocate of Vatican II's program of *ressourcement* and *aggiornamento*.[4] And here Taylor rejoins Rahner—and (perhaps to his surprise), Pope Benedict XVI.

The Christic Center of Faith

A Secular Age does not merely analyze the challenges believers face; it suggestively indicates a way forward. I have found four themes in Taylor that are remarkably consonant with the spiritual-theological vision and teaching of Benedict XVI. First, both concur that Christianity cannot be reduced to moralism, but that it opens upon an apprehension of transcendent reality. As Benedict insisted in his inaugural encyclical, *Deus Caritas Est*: "The beginning of Christian existence is not an ethical decision or a sublime idea, but rather the encounter with an event, with a person who gives life a new goal and, at the same time, a sure growth."[5]

Charles Taylor and Pope Benedict do not construe such "experience" in a subjectivist way, nor do they reduce it to private "feelings." For both, the experience in question is profoundly relational; thus the fittingness of terms like "encounter" or "apprehension." The subject encounters a reality other than self, a "deeper reality" that is "life-changing."[6] Thus the experience in question transcends moralism and verges upon "mysticism" in Rahner's sense of the word.

Second, the heart of that vision is the incarnation of God in Jesus Christ. In no other of his books is Taylor's Christian commitment so in evidence as in *A Secular Age*. He writes:

> At the heart of orthodox Christianity, seen in terms of communion, is the coming of God through Christ into a personal relation with disciples, and beyond them others, eventually ramifying through the church to humanity as a whole. God establishes the new relationship with us by loving us, in a way we cannot unaided love each other.[7]

Late in the book, in the crucial concluding chapter, "Conversions," Taylor contends: "We have to struggle to recover a sense of what the Incarnation can mean."[8]

I think it right to say that the whole of Pope Benedict's pastoral-theological program was an intense effort to recover, for contemporary men and women, "a sense of what the Incarnation can mean." From his classic *Introduction to Christianity*, through the three volumes of *Jesus of Nazareth*, to his masterful homilies and catecheses, Joseph Ratzinger has been single minded and single hearted in pursuing this quest. His goal has been to help his readers and hearers "realize" (in John Henry Newman's rich sense of the word) the meaning and implications of the incarnation. T. S. Eliot, in a memorable verse, reminds us that incarnation is "the hint half guessed, the gift half understood."[9]

In speaking and writing about Vatican II many focus almost exclusively upon the "breakthroughs" the council effected: Episcopal collegiality, religious liberty, dialogue among the world's religions. They seem to consider the council's Christological statements to be expressions of the church's perennial heritage that "goes without saying." But I insist that the four Constitutions of Vatican II are Christologically charged, fresh realizations and celebrations of the church's Lord and the world's Savior. They are the fruit of the council's profoundest re-Sourcement: its renewed discovery of the Christian faith's enlivening Source, Jesus Christ, and his significance for the modern world. Thus they orient all our prayer and thought to "what the incarnation can mean." Benedict XVI has firmly grasped and tirelessly furthered the council's Christological mandate.

A third theme, prominent in both Taylor and Pope Benedict, is that of "transformation." Both analyze at some depth the predicament that humanity faces in realizing its aspiration to the good, to "human flourishing." So often these hopes are derailed by what seems to be an almost congenital propensity to self-centeredness and self-deception. Causes, perhaps worthy in themselves, too easily become absolutized and opponents turned into enemies. Hostility and violence frequently follow in their wake.

Taylor employs a suggestive term to depict humankind's plight: he speaks of "excarnation." By it he signifies man and woman's uneasiness with being "in the flesh:" dependent, vulnerable, at the last destined to die. Death avoidance can become a whole program of life, both for an individual and for a culture. What makes this dis-ease before death particularly malevolent is that it can so easily transmute into scapegoating and death dealing. The Bible's placement of the episode of Cain and Abel at the beginnings of the human story has proved tragically prescient of the history that followed—down to our own day.

Taylor entitles the last chapter of *A Secular Age* "Conversions." In it he celebrates a number of individuals who have resisted the excarnational pulls of their time and have come to a new affirmation of incarnational faith. They have thus opened themselves to "the further, greater transformation which Christian faith holds out." He goes on to characterize this further transformation in terms derived from the Christian mystical tradition: "the raising of human life to the divine (theosis)."[10]

Pope Benedict, of course, also puts "conversion" at the heart of his teaching and preaching. One could cite passages from any number of his writings and sermons. Here is one representative example: "the liberation of man consists in his being freed from himself and, in relinquishing himself, truly finding himself." Benedict goes on: "Such a philosophy of freedom and love is, at the same time, a philosophy of conversion, of going out from oneself, of transformation; it is, therefore, also a philosophy of community and history . . ."[11] Such conversion is the antidote to excarnation.

This quotation from the pope introduces the fourth theme that he and Taylor share in common: the theme of "communion." In presenting witnesses who have broken out of modernity's immanentist confinement, Taylor accords a special place to the French poet and thinker, Charles Péguy. Péguy, who returned to the practice of the Catholicism in which he was raised, had a profound sense that "the spiritual is always incarnate" and that the individual is upheld and sustained by a chain of witnesses extending through the centuries: tradition in its most living form. As Taylor says, for Péguy, "the crucial concept here is communion, the 'joining of hands,' in other words the communion of saints to which we are all connected."[12] Taylor very much endorses this conviction of the importance of "communion" for Christianity: inseparably communion with God through Christ and, in Christ, communion with one's fellows.

This persuasion is also shared by Benedict XVI. As a theologian he develops more fully than does Taylor the trinitarian ground of this communion, both in the very life of God and in God's purpose for human salvation. Benedict's studies of Saint Augustine led him to prize Augustine's notion of the "*totus Christus*:" the "whole Christ," encompassing both Christ the Head and we the members of Christ. In an early essay, from 1961, Joseph Ratzinger wrote: "Following Christ . . . demands over and over again the personal risk of searching for him, of walking with him, but at the same time it means ceasing to build a wall around oneself, giving oneself over into the unity of 'the whole Christ,' the *totus Christus*, as Augustine beautifully puts it."[13]

Fifty years after writing that early essay, Pope Benedict repeated his steadfast conviction. In a catechesis offered in Saint Peter's Square in October 2012, he told the people gathered there: "The dialogue that God establishes with each one of us, and we with him in prayer, always includes a 'with.' It is impossible to pray to God in an individualistic manner. In liturgical prayer, especially the Eucharist and—formed by the liturgy—in every prayer, we do not only speak as individuals but on the contrary enter into the 'we' of the church that prays. And we must transform our 'I,' entering into this 'we.' "[14]

The themes of transformation and communion are so interconnected in Benedict's vision that he understands transformation as the paschal passage from the isolated "ego" to the new self in communion with Christ and with all one's brothers and sisters. An especially salient expression of this vision is found in his second encyclical, *Spe Salvi*, where Benedict audaciously writes: "Our hope is always essentially also hope for others; only thus is it truly hope for me too. As Christians we should never limit ourselves to asking: how can I save myself? We should also ask: what can I do in order that others may be saved and that for them too the star of hope may rise? Then I will have done my utmost for my own personal salvation as well."[15]

The Poetry of Faith

A final sensitivity common to both Benedict XVI and Charles Taylor deserves mention. It is their conviction of the need for a personally appropriated, poetically refined language with which to speak (always inadequately) of the Mystery in whom we live and move and have our being. The perennial risk is for religious language to become hardened into the merely formulaic, losing its mystagogic thrust.

That is why poets like Gerard Manley Hopkins and Charles Péguy assume such importance for Taylor. Hopkins' poetry evokes a sacramental world that is "charged with the grandeur of God." Péguy sings of the larger, more encompassing reality of divine-human communion. Both craft "a new subtler language."[16] Certainly not many can match such poetic genius. But we can all sit in the school of the poets to be tutored by them how better to express, in the words of Hopkins, "the dearest freshness deep down things." We can learn to guard against the deadening cliché that coarsens rather than celebrates Mystery.[17]

In a similar manner, the young Joseph Ratzinger railed against merely rote preaching. He laments: "Perhaps nothing in recent decades or even centuries has done more harm to preaching than the loss of credibility that it incurred by merely handing on formulas that were no longer the living property of those who were proclaiming them."[18] More than mere exhortation, Benedict provided in his homilies concrete paradigms of preaching done with theological depth and linguistic suppleness.

These themes, insights, and sensitivities of Benedict XVI and Charles Taylor provide important orientation and guidance for the New Evangelization. The following chapters will now seek to ponder and probe dimensions and implications of the Christic Center which is the very heart of the Good News. Two passages from the First Letter of Peter can, therefore, bring this "introduction" to a close and serve as prelude for the reflections to come.

Peter writes to an early Christian community concerning their faith in Christ Jesus and the love they bear him: "Although you have not seen him, you love him. And, even though you do not see him now, you believe in him and you rejoice with indescribable and glorious joy, for you are receiving the outcome of your faith, the salvation of your souls" (1 Pet 1:8-9). He then goes on to admonish them: "In your hearts sanctify Christ as Lord. Always be ready to make your defense to anyone who demands from you an account [*logos*] of the hope that is in you" (1 Pet 3:15). That hope is founded upon the crucified and risen Christ and Christians' love-relation to him. One may equally well say, "Always be ready to give an account of the love that is in you!" That *logos*, that "account" of our love, is the permanent core of Christian theology.[19]

The Image of Christ in the Basilica of Saint Mary Magdalene, Vézelay, France

Chapter One

The Originality and Uniqueness of Jesus the Christ

I first saw this image of the risen Christ bestowing the Holy Spirit upon the apostles as a nineteen-year-old college student. Since I first saw it, this extraordinary stone carving has been a beacon for my theological reflection and spiritual contemplation.

The small town of Vézelay is in northwestern Burgundy, on the ancient pilgrimage route to Santiago de Compostella. A magnificent church was built there in the early twelfth century in Romanesque style. The narthex, or porch area of the church, has a central door leading into the main part of the basilica. This is crowned by the splendid depiction in stone of the risen Christ from whose outsized hands the rays of the Holy Spirit are poured out upon the apostles.

The regal face of Christ has penetrating eyes as though he sees into the hearts of those entering the church, a look that both challenges and beckons. I spoke above of Christ's large hands, but in fact there is only one hand, the other being lost to the ravages of time or revolution. The impression conveyed is that the apostles, and by extension, we ourselves, are Christ's other hand, sent to spread the Gospel into the world.

Many years after that initial visit, I purchased a recording of the *Suites for Cello* of Johann Sebastian Bach, by the great Russian master Mstislav Rostropovich. In the notes to the recording Rostropovich confesses that he had waited to record these sublime works until he felt he had attained a requisite artistic and even spiritual maturity. He finally decided in 1991 that the time had come. But he wanted the record-

ing to be made in the most evocative and spiritually inspiring setting he knew. For this reason he chose to record them in the Basilica at Vézelay.

To enter the Basilica, having passed under the great image of the risen Christ, radiating the Holy Spirit, is to enter the new world of grace that calls to transformation and new life.

Prelude: Singing Hymns to Christ as God

In his fine book, *The Spirit of Early Christian Thought: Seeking the Face of God*, Robert Wilken writes:

> The church gave men and women a new love, Jesus Christ, a person who inspired their actions and held their affections. This was a love unlike others. For it was not only that Jesus was a wise teacher or a compassionate human being who reached out to the sick and needy, or even that he patiently suffered abuse and calumny and died a cruel death, but that after his death God had raised him from the dead to a new life. He who once was dead now lives. The Resurrection of Jesus is the central fact of Christian devotion and the ground of all Christian thinking.[1]

What was the case for the early Christians remains the case for all subsequent generations who undertake the challenge and responsibility of evangelization. Jesus Christ inspires the actions of Christians and holds their affections, he can be the subject of their unique love and devotion, because he is not merely a figure of the past who underwent a brutal death by crucifixion. Jesus

Christ is risen and present to the community, especially in its gathering for worship. According to the Roman governor Pliny, writing to Emperor Trajan, it was here, in their liturgical celebrations, that early Christians sang "hymns to Christ as God."[2] So it is today.

One of the most noteworthy achievements in ecumenical theological discussion since Vatican II has been the realization that Scripture and Tradition are not separate spheres but are vitally interconnected. Scripture itself is the normative and privileged expression of the Tradition that comes from the Apostles. Tradition is both the source and the bearer of the apostolic witness embodied in Scripture. A salient example of this interconnection may be found in the so-called "Christological hymns" of the New Testament.

These hymns, in the view of scholars, antedate their appearances in the writings of the New Testament. They seem to be hymns actually sung in the communities, during their festive celebrations. They have then been incorporated into the written texts, almost as reminders and points of reference for the Good News that is being narrated and taught. The most notable examples are found in the "prologue" to the Gospel of John, in the second chapter of Saint Paul's Letter to the Philippians, and in the first chapter of the Letter to the Colossians. Such hymns, or their like, may well have been the subject of Pliny's reference.[3]

What is remarkable about them is that they bear witness to a truly exalted sense of the identity and salvific significance of Jesus as Messiah and Lord. They represent what some call "first theology"—the lived celebration and symbol-laden interpretation of the unique figure of Jesus—that precedes and grounds the more conceptually elaborated "second theology" of the early fathers and councils of the church. Even more remarkable is that the Christological claims, given exultant voice in these hymns, concern a figure who, within living memory, had undergone shameful and scandalous crucifixion as a common criminal.

Though volumes have been written upon each of the Christological hymns, let us consider the one embedded in the Letter to the Colossians as a crucial confession of the originality and uniqueness of Jesus.

The introduction, with which the author of Colossians prefaces the hymn, takes the form of an exhortation to give thanks to God the Father. For "he rescued us from the power of darkness and transferred us to the kingdom of his beloved Son in whom we have redemption, the forgiveness of our sins" (Col 1:13-14). Then the hymn itself further identifies this Son who has effected believers' reconciliation and is the one through whom they receive grace and peace.

> He is the image of the invisible God
> > the firstborn of all creation.
> For in him were created all things in heaven and on earth,
> > the visible and invisible
> > whether thrones or dominions or principalities or powers;
> All things were created through him and for him.
> He is before all things
> > and in him all things hold together.
> He is the head of the body, the church.
> He is the beginning, the firstborn from the dead
> > so that in all things he himself might have primacy.
> For in him all the fullness of God was pleased to dwell
> > and through him to reconcile all things to himself
> > whether on earth or in heaven
> > making peace through the blood of his cross. (Col 1:15-20)[4]

The fundamental and perennial Christological question is the one Jesus posed at Caesarea Philippi to his first and to all subsequent disciples: "Who do you say I am?" (Mark 8:29). The hymn in the Letter to the Colossians, sung by early Christians, responds to this question in astonishing ways. Clearly the one who is con-

fessed is the one who shed his blood on the cross, thereby reconciling all things to God. We have grown so accustomed to singing and speaking of being redeemed by Christ's death that the strangeness of the affirmation has become muted. Yet the scandalous claim remains: the execution of a Jew, in a remote province of the Roman Empire, has somehow effected the salvation of all.

Adding to the astonishment is the hymn's claim that in the all too human face of this executed criminal we can glimpse the very image of the invisible God. God's whole plan for creation is embodied in him. Indeed, in view of him all creation finds its meaning and fulfillment. That fulfillment is inaugurated in the resurrection of Jesus from the dead, "the firstborn from the dead," as the hymn proclaims, or, as Saint Paul professes to the Corinthians, "the first-fruits of those who have fallen asleep" (1 Cor 15:20). A new age has dawned, the new creation has begun.

The New Adam

God's victory achieved in Christ continues to reap the promised harvest in the church of which the resurrected Lord is the head, the ongoing source of new life. Jesus Christ continues to fashion those who believe in him into the new persons who have left behind death-dealing ways and are being perfected by their loving, wholehearted devotion to God and the service of the brethren. Indeed, God's saving purpose for humankind is that the One who is the true image of the Father should be the exemplar and empowering source for the ingathering of the many into "the Kingdom of the beloved Son."

Though the term, as such, is not found in Colossians, the reality celebrated may be fittingly called "Christification."[5] For, after quoting the hymn, the author joyfully sums up the revelation of which he is the bearer as "Christ in you: the hope of glory" (Col

1:27). And he characterizes his own apostolic ministry thus: "It is Christ whom we proclaim, admonishing everyone and teaching everyone with all wisdom, that we may present everyone perfected in Christ" (Col 1:28). Through the ages the purpose of Christian ministry is to promote the "Christification," the rebirth and ongoing transformation of all in Christ.[6]

A sense of radical newness permeates the entire New Testament. It reflects the early communities' "eschatological" conviction concerning Christ. God has acted in history in a final and definitive fashion in the life, death, and new life of Jesus and has brought to fulfillment all his promises to Israel. The Letter to the Hebrews gives canonical expression to this conviction: "God, in many and various ways, spoke to our ancestors in times past by the prophets, but in these last days he has spoken to us by a Son, whom he appointed heir of all things, through whom also he created the worlds" (Heb 1:1-2). The Greek word for "last" is *eschatos*: in these final definitive days. Thus "final" not in the quantitative sense of the world coming to an end, but in the qualitative sense of unsurpassable, eschatological fulfillment.

Saint Paul proclaims this overwhelming sense of the newness and originality of Jesus when he speaks of Jesus Christ as the "last Adam." Paul writes: "The first man, Adam, became a living being; the last Adam became a life-giving spirit" (1 Cor 15:45). Again, the Greek word used is *eschatos*: Christ is the eschatological Adam, the human intended by God from all eternity. The new eschatological age has dawned with the resurrection of Jesus from the dead, the firstborn of many brothers and sisters. The second-century bishop and theologian Saint Irenaeus of Lyons well captures the Tradition's conviction when he writes: "Christ brought all newness, bringing himself."[7]

We can further probe this "newness" by focusing not merely upon what Jesus *did*, but upon who Jesus *is*—as Irenaeus suggests: "bringing himself."

Jesus: Priest and Sacrifice

Central to the personal reality of Jesus is his attentive listening and obedience to the will of the Father. Unlike the "first Adam" and his descendants, Jesus fulfills the will of the Father to the point of affirming: "my food is to do the will of the One who sent me and to complete his work" (John 4:34). The entire Tradition meditates with awe the Synoptic account of Jesus' struggle in the Garden of Gethsemane to align perfectly his human will with that of the Father. "Abba, Father, all things are possible for you. Take this cup from me. But not what I will but what you will be done" (Mark 14:36). The "agony in the garden" became one of the fixed points in affirming the true humanity of the Savior and his utter surrender to the Father's saving purpose. It is the ultimate testimony to the words he taught his disciples to pray: "Father, your will be done on earth as in heaven" (Matt 6:10).

We can ponder still further the uniqueness of Jesus' very selfhood. Not only is there a "moral" coincidence of wills between Jesus and his heavenly Father, the "newness" the Tradition proclaims is deeper yet. One may rightly call it "ontological." The very being of Jesus manifests the true humanity that God desires. Jesus is the faithful covenant partner who images perfectly God's love and fidelity. There is revealed in Jesus that *new relational self* who is totally *for* God and totally *at the service of* his brothers and sisters.[8] And his service is himself: "the bread that I will give is my flesh for the life of the world" (John 6:51).

For this reason the Letter to the Hebrews proclaims Jesus to be the one High Priest whose priestly service is the offering of himself. The sacrifice of Jesus fulfills and transcends all the intimations and foreshadowings present in God's history with Israel.[9] He thus initiates the new and everlasting covenant. The liturgical tradition acknowledges this in speaking of Jesus as both priest and sacrifice. It follows the Letter to the Hebrews in gratefully confessing: "when Christ came as high priest of the good things

that have come to be, passing through the greater and more perfect tent (not made with hands, that is, not of this creation), he
entered once for all into the sanctuary, not with the blood of goats
and calves, but with his own blood, thus achieving eternal redemption" (Heb 9:11-12). The definitive and unsurpassable Good
News is that "we have been sanctified by the offering of the body
of Jesus Christ once for all" (Heb 10:10) who, "being made perfect
became the source of eternal salvation for all who obey him,
designated by God high priest according to the order of Melchi-
sedech" (Heb 5:9-10). Jesus fulfills and embodies priesthood in
his own person.[10]

Jesus as Concrete Universal

The Colossians hymn (as we have seen) celebrates the primacy
of Jesus in both creation and redemption: the firstborn of all
creation, the firstborn from the dead. How are we to join this
universalist, even cosmic, confession of the priority of Jesus
Christ with the concrete particularity of his existence at a deter-
minate place and time, heir of a specific religious tradition? Teilhard de Chardin wrestled with this question throughout his life,
seeking to bring together his deep Christian faith with his commitment to modern science. He wrote poignantly in his spiritual
classic, *The Divine Milieu*: "Is the Christ of the Gospels, imagined
and loved within the dimensions of a Mediterranean world, ca-
pable of still embracing and still forming the center of our pro-
digiously expanded universe?"[11]

Much of the theological labor of the great twentieth-century
Catholic theologian Hans Urs von Balthasar pivots around this
question of Christ's unsurpassable uniqueness. He speaks of Jesus
Christ as "the concrete universal." Jesus is the one who takes upon
himself the sin of the whole world, allowing all its death-dealing
hostility to overwhelm him. By entering into the void of God-

refusal and God-hatred, Jesus brings God's presence and love into the depths of human alienation and abandonment. But the price is literally heart breaking: "from his side there flowed blood and water" (John 19:34).[12]

Some are drawn to ask, in diverse situations of their lives, "what would Jesus do?" In a more sustained way, believers seek to "take on the mind of Christ," as Saint Paul exhorts the Philippians (Phil 2:5)—just before he quotes the Christological hymn that celebrates Jesus' kenotic (self-emptying) manner of existence which Christians are to emulate.

> Though he was in the form of God, Jesus did not consider equality with God something to be held on to, but emptied himself taking on the form of a slave. And being found in human form, he humbled himself, becoming obedient unto death, even death on a cross. (Phil 2:6-8)

This *self-emptying pattern* characterizes the historical life and ministry of Jesus, culminating in his sacrifice upon the cross under Pontius Pilate (as the Creed insistently recalls).

This paschal pattern characterizes God's grace *universally*, wherever it is found. Whether within or outside the empirical Christian community, God's grace always bears a paschal shape. Jesus, in his death and resurrection, concretely enacts and embodies God's universal promise. He has himself become the new and everlasting covenant. Hence von Balthasar's insistence that Jesus is "the concrete universal:" God's universal saving will accomplished in his very person.

Vatican II's Pastoral Constitution, *Gaudium et Spes*, affirms: the Holy Spirit "offers to all the possibility of being participants, in a way known only to God, in Christ's paschal mystery" (22). The book of Revelation already intimated this universality when it speaks (in a dense and evocative passage) of "the lamb slain since the foundation of the world" (Rev 13:8). Self-giving love forms the very pattern, the *logos*, of the universe created and redeemed by God.

Jesus' Eucharistic Imagination

As we consider the uniqueness and originality of Jesus in the context of the New Evangelization, here is another meditative path to ponder. Though we often speak of Jesus' "mind" or his "will," we seldom reflect on or speak of Jesus' "imagination." It is helpful, however, to muse upon imagination as the source of the creative vision that inspires great works of art. Think of the supreme artists from whose imaginations have sprung the seminal works that have nourished and enhanced our spirits through the ages: the plays of Sophocles and Shakespeare, the paintings of Raphael and Caravaggio, the sculpture of Michelangelo and Bernini, the novels of Dostoyevsky and Dickens, the music of Bach and Mozart. These and their peers have given us radiant, even life-transforming glimpses of the creative power of God.

Jesus gathers up and transcends them all. For he has imagined—and *realized in himself*—a world redeemed. All the others who have created lasting works of beauty and goodness are distinguishable from their works. But Jesus *is* his work.[13] He is the redeemer, the savior. His whole being is to be for God and humankind, reconciling the two in his own body, as the Tradition hymns with wonder and gratitude. Jesus' defining passion is his passion for communion, the New Testament *koinônia*. His consuming passion is to bring men and women into communion with God and (inseparably) with one another; to lead them into the promised land of God's Kingdom.[14]

If we were to characterize succinctly the imagination of Jesus, we could speak of it, then, as a "eucharistic imagination" impelled by his *passion for communion*. This passion for communion energized the entire life of Jesus. Jesus' teaching and healings, his meals with poor and rich, Pharisees and publicans, even his challenges and disputes transpired in the Spirit whose goal is ever communion/*koinônia*. Jesus' passion for communion, his compassion for all the sick, lost, and alienated, culminated with the Last Supper and the cross. Supper and cross mutually illuminate one another. They represent the consummation of the new order Jesus was intent on instituting, the new eucharistic world he was bringing into being.

The Fear of Death

Believers often pose or are confronted with the question: why the cross? Could not God have redeemed and restored humanity in some less radical, less extreme way, at far less costly a price? Without desiring to domesticate the Mystery, one might venture a modest discernment. Returning to Charles Taylor's suggestive depiction of the human plight in terms of "excarnation," can we trace the roots of this inveterate temptation to humankind's fear of death? Might it be fear of death that drives humanity's impulse to excarnation? We erect ego-protective defenses to shield ourselves from the threat of death and diminishment.

The Letter to the Hebrews contains an intriguing passage that lends support to this perspective. "Therefore, since, the children share flesh and blood, Jesus himself shared the same, so that through death he might destroy the one who has the power of death, that is, the devil, and free those who all their lives long were held in slavery by fear of death" (Heb 2:14-15). Taylor himself does not probe to any great extent this "thanatological" (from the Greek word for "death") reading of the human predicament. But many artists and poets show a keen sensitivity to the place that fear of death holds in distorting our life and thwarting our yearning for communion. One recalls, for instance, Walker

Percy's final novel, *The Thanatos Syndrome* and Andre Dubus' superb essay, "On Charon's Wharf."[15]

It is crucial, however, to stress two points in analyzing the "fear of death." First, it is not suggested that this fear is itself "pathological." It is instinctive and can bespeak a fitting reaction to a perceived danger. The important issue is what this fear leads to, how it affects our decisions and conduct. It can all too often prompt us to retreat into a protective shell, even an impermeable fortification, thereby depriving oneself of light and air, like a tomb. At the extreme it can turn death dealing, as in the case of Cain, eliminating that which is perceived as threat.[16]

This suggests the second important point in an analysis of the fear of death. The "death" in question need not be construed, in the first instance, as the termination of physical life. Rather, it embraces all those situations which mirror "death:" any diminution of our sense of self. Suffering, hatred, enmity, rejection, betrayal all carry the "scent" of death to our threatened selves, as so many of the psalms lament. And closely allied with our recoil before the onslaught of these deadly diminishments is our tendency to self-deception: the lies we tell to ourselves as well as to others. The lie of self-deception is so often the evasion of a truth too painful and deadly to bear.[17]

The drama of the Gospel of John lies in just this combat between life and death, truth and lie. This is presented most vividly in the judgment scene between Jesus and Pilate: between him who embodies the authority of truth and him who wields the power to inflict death (John 18:28–19:16). In John's gospel Jesus speaks words that shock, but they may be a "shock therapy" that promotes salutary awakening. He exclaims, "the devil was a murderer from the beginning . . . he is a liar and the father of lies" (John 8:44). Jesus, by contrast, bears witness to the truth of the Father of life. Indeed, Jesus himself is "the truth and the life" and we only have access to the Father through him (John 14:6).

The Victory of the Cross and Resurrection

If, then, fear of death plays so decisive a role in the human spiritual drama and, ultimately, in our foundational relation to the God of life, distorting that relation through mistrust and disobedience, could the work of the Savior be finally fruitful unless it dealt with this human predicament at its very root? From this vantage, well-meaning reactions to a mistaken depiction of the cross as placating an "angry" God, risk ignoring the true depth of human need and the costliness of salvation. Certainly Jesus acted out of love; but his action was to embrace, not reject, the cross. It was the devil that tempted toward an easier way. And it was Peter who falsely urged upon Jesus a different path for the Messiah.

Christian faith and liturgy contend that Jesus entered into battle with the forces of darkness, not only the more evident manifestations of sin, but their deeper, demonic roots. The gospels celebrate this victory of the Stronger one who triumphs by binding Satan (see Matt 12:24-32). Christ's death on the cross is in no sense a "payment" offered to appease the justice of God or to assuage God's wrath. It is, rather, the supreme revelation of the depth of God's love and the terrible consequences and tragedy of human sin. But the revelation occurs precisely in the death embraced, which is not merely an unfortunate consequence of Jesus' ministry, but its salvific fulfillment.

In face of a widespread tendency to relativize the centrality of the cross, the theologian William Frazier, in a provocative article, expresses succinctly the crucial issue: "Here is the correct way to connect the three mysteries of love, obedience and death: God saved the world through the loving and obedient death of Jesus, and this is a far cry from having done so through the love and obedience of Jesus' death."[18] The accent falls upon the death of Jesus—certainly entered into through loving obedience—but freely embraced in order that death itself might be transformed and the Kingdom of life established.

The glorious victory of Christ over sin and death is gained not by death-dealing reprisals, but by entering into the very throes of death and confronting the fear that had held humankind captive. The great "Sequence," proclaimed on Easter Sunday, marvels that "death and life strove in stupendous combat; the author of life died, yet reigns alive." The cross, in this light, is the final and definitive exorcism which renders the powers powerless. So the church chants: "*Ave, O Crux, spes unica!*" ("Hail, O Cross, our sole hope!")

Saint Paul places the cross at the very heart of his proclamation of the Good News of Jesus Christ. He reminds the Corinthians: "When I came to you, proclaiming the testimony of God, brothers and sisters, I did not come with facile speech or facile wisdom. Rather, I resolved to know nothing among you, save Jesus Christ and him crucified" (1 Cor 2:1-2). This "word of the cross," this heralding of Christ crucified, is, indeed, "a scandal to Jews and folly to Gentiles, but to those who are called, Jews and Greeks alike, Christ is God's power and God's wisdom" (1 Cor 1:23-24).

Christ's crucifixion is ultimately attributable to human sinfulness. Paul quotes the tradition he himself had received: "Christ died for our sins in accordance with the scriptures" (1 Cor 15:3). By the death and resurrection of Jesus Messiah the power of sin is confronted at its root and its stranglehold upon human beings is at last overcome. Hence Paul, transforming the words of Hosea, can boast: "Death has been swallowed up in victory. Where, death, is your victory? Where is your sting?" and joyfully exult: "Death's sting is sin, and sin's power is the law. But thanks be to God who has given us the victory through our Lord, Jesus Christ" (1 Cor 15: 55-56).

Jesus' death for our sake would, of course, have been futile and fruitless without his resurrection from the dead on the third day. Paul is unequivocal: "if Christ has not been raised, then our preaching is in vain and your faith is in vain" (1 Cor 15:14). It is crucial to hold Christ's death and resurrection in tensive unity. Without his loving death, humankind remains alienated and unredeemed; without his resurrection humankind does not receive Christ's own Spirit and enter into the new creation.

Often the Christian West focused one-sidedly upon the cross, neglecting or losing the joy and hope of the resurrection.[19] It is imperative to do justice in Christian living and Christian thinking to the integrity of the paschal mystery of Christ. Only through his death and resurrection do we come to share in God's own life. Only through faith in Christ crucified and risen can we joyfully exclaim with Paul: "I am sure that neither death nor life, neither angels nor principalities, not things present nor things to come, neither powers nor height nor depth, not anything else in all creation will be able to separate us from the love of God in Christ Jesus our Lord" (Rom 8:38-39).

Jesus Christ, by his cross and resurrection, has transformed the height and breadth and length and depth of human existence into Eucharist. He has made all of human experience a thanksgiving offering to God on behalf of the many. His cross is the consummation of his passion for communion to the point of taking on himself the sins of the world. His resurrection is the beginning of the new creation, the "eighth day," the "Lord's Day," of eucharistic celebration. Resurrection, then, is the end, the goal of incarnation: humanity fully transformed and glorified in God. Whether in the first century or the twenty-first, this Good News is the heart of evangelization.

Jesus Is Salvation

From the perspective of "soteriology"—reflection upon the meaning of salvation—Jesus does much more than provide an example, showing humans the way to salvation. He is himself salvation: he creates the way to at-one-ment, union with God. His risen body is the sphere of salvation into which believers are incorporated through the Holy Spirit. To be "in Christ" is to enter God's kingdom in the company of a multitude of brothers and sisters.

In his *Lectures on Justification*, John Henry Newman expresses this with rhetorical precision. "Christ came for this very purpose, to gather together in one all the elements of good dispersed throughout the world, to make them his own, to illuminate them with himself, to reform and refashion them into himself. He came to make a new and better beginning of all things than Adam had been, and to be a fountainhead from which all good henceforth might flow."[20] The "originality" of Jesus is that he is the origin, the fountainhead from which the new creation, the new redeemed humanity springs.

A theology in service of the New Evangelization must be one in which the uniqueness and originality of Jesus is probed with creativity and imagination. I have tried to sketch some approaches to the inexhaustible newness of Jesus who, in the words of Irenaeus already quoted, "brought all newness, by bringing himself." Rich symbols like "new creation," "New Adam," "new covenant" must be newly appropriated and imaginatively presented so as to attract hearts and minds searching for meaning and purpose in their lives and relationships. The beauty, goodness, and truth of Jesus must lay hold of us as we strive to fathom the extent of the transformation to which he summons us. Jesus' passion for communion and his eucharistic imagination must fire our passion and enkindle our imagination, not only in the enthusiasm of a first conversion, but throughout the transfigurative journey of discipleship.

Already/Not Yet

The new creation has already begun in the resurrection of Christ and is spreading in those who have been incorporated into Christ by baptism and who are nourished by the Eucharist. But, though the eschatological age has dawned with the risen Christ, his victory has yet to be fully realized in humanity and the world. An "eschatological tension"—the tension of the "already" and the "not yet"—characterizes the New Testament witness. It receives poignant expression in Paul's Letter to the Romans. "We know that the whole creation has been groaning together in the throes of childbirth until now. And we ourselves as well, who have the first fruit of the Spirit groan in eager expectation of our filial adoption and the redemption of our body" (Rom 8:22-23).

We have indeed received the Spirit as first fruit; however, the full crop has not yet been harvested. Nevertheless, our hope remains secure because it is founded upon what the Father has accomplished in raising Jesus. As the First Letter of John proclaims: "Beloved, we are now children of God; it has not yet become manifest what we shall be. But we do know that, when Christ appears, we shall be like him, for we shall see him as he is" (1 John 3:2).

As suggested above, salvation, at its core, is not something Jesus brings, but *who Jesus is*, the new Adam, the beginning of the new creation. So for us, salvation is not merely a new situation, however desirable that may be. It is a new self being transformed into the likeness of Christ. To be saved is to enter into the body of Christ as a living member. We will explore further implications of this in our next chapters. But at this point it is important to see that this incorporation of persons into Christ is the work of the Holy Spirit.

Already in the preface, we had occasion to insist, quoting Yves Congar, that Christology and pneumatology are inseparable in the Gospel tradition. Congar further writes, "the vigor of a lived pneumatology is to be found in Christology: there is only one body which the Spirit builds up and quickens, and that is the body of Christ."[21] John Henry Newman, in one of his sermons, expresses concisely the inseparable missions of Christ and the Spirit. He says, "The Holy Spirit does not so come that Christ does not come, but rather the Spirit comes that Christ may come in his coming." And he adds, "The Holy Spirit causes . . . the indwelling of Christ in the heart. Thus the Spirit does not take the place of Christ in the soul, but secures that place to Christ."[22]

Since Christ and the Spirit together effect human salvation, bestowing on humanity the very life of God, the tradition rejoices that Christians themselves share the Son's filial relation to the Father: "to those who received him he gave power to become children of God" (John 1:12). The experience of new life through Christ in the Holy Spirit issues in a new sense of God: a God who is triune. It is the community's discernment of the uniqueness of Jesus that presses Christian thought toward the distinctive confession of the triune God.

Rublev Icon of the Holy Trinity

Chapter Two

"The Love that Moves the Sun and the Other Stars"

Icons have been central to Christian worship and prayer, especially in the Christian East, for over sixteen hundred years. In the Eastern church they have an almost sacramental significance, venerated with tender devotion. Perhaps no icon is better known and more theologically rich than Rublev's icon of the Holy Trinity.

Rublev's fifteenth-century masterpiece is the heir of a long tradition of iconic depiction of the Holy Trinity. The biblical background, however, is from the Old Testament. Thus the icon is sometimes referred to as "The Hospitality of Abraham." It derives from the account in chapter 18 of the book of Genesis where the Lord appeared to Abraham in the guise of three young men (angel-messengers of the Most High). Abraham begs the visitors to stay and offers them food and drink for the journey. They in turn promise that Sarah, though aged, would bear the son, long promised by God.

From early days Christians read the scene in trinitarian terms, seeing it as an anticipation of the full revelation of the Trinity in the New Testament. Further, in the meal prepared by Abraham, they saw a foreshadowing of the Eucharist offered by Christ. It is generally agreed that, as we face the icon, the figure on the left is the Father, the figure at the center is the Son, and the figure on the right is the Holy Spirit. Each bears in his hand the staff of coequal authority, but each person is distinguished by posture and gesture. What makes Rublev's depiction stand apart from other representations is not only the beauty of the composition and the figures, but the dynamic interrelationship among the three that he achieves.

The figure of the Son is shown with right hand extended in blessing, the two fingers also testifying to his divine and human nature. The meal served by Abraham has been transformed into the Eucharist of Christ which it prefigured. Here the importance of the unoccupied fourth side of the table/altar becomes apparent. It is the space reserved for the beholder who is invited to become a participant, to enter into the communion of the Trinity through partaking in the eucharistic meal.

The narrow rectangle on the front of the altar represents the four corners of the world to which the invitation goes forth. However, the invitation, though free, is not without cost. Jesus says: "Narrow is the gate and hard the way that leads to life" (Matt 7:14). The

icon was meant to be placed in a liturgical setting where the Eucharist is celebrated. Thus it serves as both invitation and caution. It calls out: "holy gifts for God's holy people." Yet, as St. Paul urges: "Whoever eats the bread or drinks the cup of the Lord unworthily will be guilty of the body and blood of the Lord. So let each examine him or herself and then eat of the bread and drink of the cup" (1 Cor 11:27-28).

In addition to its liturgical placement, the icon of the Holy Trinity is a powerful stimulus to personal prayer of a more contemplative nature. One can position oneself before the icon, in the open place at the table, rejoicing in the love of the Trinity for us. While praying before the icon, we can bring to grateful remembrance those who are intimately close to us and meditatively imagine them next to us on the left and right, both those living on earth and those fully living with the Lord.

Henri Nouwen wrote a lovely book in which he presents four icons and reflects prayerfully on each. He aptly titles his meditation on the Rublev icon of the Holy Trinity: "Living in the House of Love."[1]

Prelude: Dante's Journey of Transformation

Dante's *Divine Comedy* is the greatest and most comprehensive poetic expression of the Catholic vision of reality. It is at once intensely personal and audaciously cosmic in scope. Its form and content together form an intricate unity. As is well known, the poem comprises three *cantiche*: *Inferno*, *Purgatorio*, and *Paradiso*. Hence the architecture of the *Commedia* is triadic. Moreover, each *cantica* has thirty-three cantos that constitute the dramatic units of the whole and reinforce the poem's trinitarian structure. An introductory canto joins the remaining ninety-nine to bring the total to one hundred cantos. In Medieval numerology ten was considered the perfect number: the Trinity squared plus the unity of God. And one hundred is the perfect number squared. Thus the very form manifests the fullness of the vision the poem offers.

But there are further formal features of the poem that bring us even nearer to its existential content. Each canto is comprised of tercets, three-line verses. In addition Dante employs *terza rima* as his rhyme scheme. Thus the final word of the second line of each tercet finds rhyming echo in the endings of the first and third line of the following tercet. Hence the formal structure is: aba/bcb/cdc etcetera. Here are the famous opening tercets of the *Inferno* to provide a sense of the rhyme:

> Nel mezzo del cammin di nostra vita
> mi ritrovai per una selva oscura
> che la diritta via era smaritta.
>
> Ahi quanto a dir qual era è cosa dura
> esta selva selvaggia e aspra e forte
> che nel pensier rinnova la paura![2]

What does this formal characteristic reveal about the poem's existential intent? In a fine article, "The Significance of *Terza Rima*," the Dante scholar John Freccero points to the unique feature of the form as both remembering the past and anticipating the future. In the above verses, *dura* echoes *oscura* and inclines toward *paura*. Thus *terza rima* propels a dynamic movement that images the existential movement of the pilgrim's transformative journey. Poetic form and theological substance support one another.[3]

Indeed, the form of *terza rima* reproduces musically the trinitarian content of the entire poem. Through his long and arduous journey, Dante the pilgrim is guided and sustained by the trinitarian rhythm of the cantos until he reaches the consummating vision of the Trinity in Paradiso 33. *Terza rima* is the cantus firmus of the journey of transformation, until the pilgrim's being becomes fully attuned to the very rhythms of God's trinitarian life.

In this regard, one feature of the *Commedia* deserves special note in its wedding of form and content. Whenever the name "Christ" is evoked, the word rhymes only with itself: "*Cristo . . . Cristo . . . Cristo.*" This three-fold repetition reveals the perfect embodiment of humanity's constitutive relation to the triune God.

The doctrine of the Trinity is not some esoteric teaching, some mathematical conundrum. It is the way that Christians tell the story of God who created and redeemed the world through Christ in the Spirit. It is the story, in Dante's words, of "the Love that moves the sun and the other stars."

Mystery

Christians often refer to the Trinity as "mystery"—and rightly so. However, too often mystery is taken to mean an insoluble puzzle or an incomprehensible reality. When presented in catechesis or preached about on "Trinity Sunday," the impression often given is that one cannot understand so one should not bother trying. The catechist or preacher then moves on to other less "mysterious" matters. The image conveyed is that of a red light, a "stop!" to understanding.

However, the true theological understanding of the mystery of the Trinity is that it is the fullness of light and life. Thus it is not so much incomprehensible as inexhaustible. We can never fully fathom the mystery, but that serves as an invitation to further exploration. Hence not a red light, but a blinking yellow light: proceed with caution and reverence. As Moses heard the voice from the burning bush: "take off your sandals, for you are treading on holy ground" (Exod 3:5).

Indeed, the joyous profession of faith in the triune God has nothing to do with a mathematic puzzle—of how one can be three and three one. Rather, the mystery proclaimed is that of the living God, whose love is the origin of all things, "visible and invisible."

The Christian sense of the Mystery of the living God is deeply rooted in the soil of Israel's faith. Israel's scriptures nourished the vision of Jesus and his early followers by narrating and celebrating the creating and redeeming deeds of God who chose Israel to be God's witness and promise to the nations.

The God of Israel

Unlike the New Testament writings, which span only some fifty years from the earliest to the latest, the books of the Old Testament embody hundreds of years of tradition and transmission. Without pretending to do full justice to the array of testimonies, from divergent historical and cultural situations, one can discern the distinctive patterns that characterize Israel's encounter with God. What emerges above all is that the initiative is God's. God's gracious will initiates and sustains all God's dealings with Israel.

We see this clearly in God's paradigmatic call of Abraham in the twelfth chapter of Genesis. In the context of Genesis, chapter

12 marks a new beginning of God's dealings with humankind. After the series of falls from grace—culminating in the fragmentation of the human race after the failed effort to pierce the heavens with the Tower of Babel—God calls forth an individual, Abraham, to embark on a new way for humanity. That way is the way of blessing: "I will bless you" and "all the communities of the earth will find blessing in you" (Gen 12:2, 3).

God's relationship with Abraham and God's promise to him are sealed by covenant. God's enduring love and fidelity are to be reciprocated by Abraham's loving obedience and trust. Through the vicissitudes of Abraham's journey of faith, Israel's own journey is exemplified and mirrored. What strikes one in the biblical account is God's condescension: God's willingness to "stoop down" in order to elevate the creature: to bless so that man and woman might become themselves sources of blessing.[4]

This generous condescension of God goes so far as to identify God's own self by reference to those with whom God enters into covenant. The eternal One assumes the name of those called into personal relation: the God of Abraham and Sarah, of Isaac and Rebecca, of Jacob and Rachel. The God of Israel's faith is preeminently personal: One who acts freely, constrained by no need, but only out of love and compassion.

This defining character of God is further manifest in one of the pinnacles of Old Testament revelation: the theophany to Moses in chapter 3 of the book of Exodus. God self-identifies as "the God of your father, the God of Abraham, the God of Isaac, the God of Jacob" (Exod 3:6). The God of the fathers, the personal God, appears in an alien land because of compassion at the plight of the Israelites. But when pressed by Moses for a yet fuller revelation of the identity of this mysterious Other, God replies: "I am who I am" (Exod 3:14).

Biblical scholars have parsed the etymology of the sacred Name, theologians have speculated upon its manifold significance. We know that the people of Israel so reverenced the re-vealed Name that they did not pronounce it when reading the text, but in its stead read "Adonai," "my Lord." It is this faith-filled practice of Israel that provides access to a further sense of the character of Israel's God. God is both mysteriously Other than the human, transcendent to all created reality, yet also mysteri-ously present, immanent to meet human need.

Throughout Israel's history this sense of awesome majesty and compassionate presence will inspire and direct the visions of prophets and the songs of psalmists. The prophet Isaiah's great vision in the temple of the thrice-holy God, before whom Isaiah confesses his sinful distance, coexists with the mission to the people upon which Isaiah is sent in God's Name (Isa 6:1-13). The Lord, hidden to mortal sight by the heavenly host, nonetheless speaks to the prophet and through the prophet to the people: "Go, say to this people!" (Isa 6:9).

One of the greatest of Israel's psalms, Psalm 139 marvels at the surpassing power of God, yet at the same time confesses God's intimate knowledge of the psalmist's very being and every thought. The eternal One is ever present. "Where can I hide from your Spirit? Where can I flee from your presence? If I ascend to the heavens, you are there; if I lie down in the nether world, you are there" (Ps 139:7-8). Yet this magnificent hymn of praise, extolling God's wondrous plan, concludes with imprecations against the wicked and prayers for their destruction—verses 19-22, unfortu-nately omitted from the Liturgy of the Hours.

I say "unfortunately omitted," because the omission obscures the fact that God's revelation to Israel is progressive. With regard to the paradigmatic figure of Abraham, God led Abraham, "edu-cated" him to a fuller apprehension of God's ways. Moses too was gradually purified (in his enduring experience of the burning bush of God's holiness) to become an apt leader of God's people. The prophets sought persistently to wean the king and the people from submission to idols to the service of the living God. Yet, as Psalm 139 shows, God's quest for the totally Just One, the One who fully embodies God's Word, is not yet achieved.

One Old Testament scholar traces this long struggle of the prophets to turn Israel and its leaders away from the pomp of power and riches toward embodying God's justice. He writes:

> The Solomonic era, instead of inaugurating God's kingdom, initiated a long period of testing and learning. For until this people could be purged of their earthly ideas of God's reign, they would continue to confuse their penultimate kingdom with God's ultimate kingdom.[5]

The catastrophe of the Temple's destruction and the exile of many of the people to Babylon in 587 BCE tested Israel's faith in an unprecedented way. Yet the great prophet known as Second Isaiah heard God's Word in an alien land and proclaimed the uniqueness of Israel's God in the face of the seeming victory of Israel's enemies. His insistent claim was that the gods of the overbearing powers are mere idols fashioned by human hands, incapable of providing lasting salvation, destined to disappear despite their temporary pomp and preening. "Thus says the Lord, King and Redeemer of Israel, the Lord of hosts: I am the first and I am the last—there is no other god" (Isa 44:6).

The Servant

Perhaps the summit of God's revelation to Israel (at least from a Christian perspective) are the four passages in Second Isaiah that have come to be known as the "Songs of the Servant."[6] They depict a figure who will be the bearer of God's salvation to the nations. The Servant (whether an individual or Israel as a whole is disputed, but the thrust of the passages points finally to an individual) is God's "chosen one" whom God will "uphold." God's purpose for the Servant is to "bring forth justice to the nations" (Isa 42:1). Through the Servant God's glory will be revealed (49:3), not only by gathering Israel to the Lord, but by being "a light to the nations" (49:6). Yet in these first songs there is already a hint that the mission of the Servant will entail suffering and rejection. "I did not hide my face from buffets and spitting" (50:6).

As in a symphony in four movements, the fourth Song of the Servant sums up what went before and introduces us into a new transcendent realm. There was no comeliness to the Servant, indeed he was despised and rejected among men (53:2, 3). "He was wounded for our offenses, crushed for our sins . . . by his wounds we are healed" (Isa 53:5). "Like a lamb he is led to slaughter, yet he remains silent and opens not his mouth" (53:7). "He was given a grave among evildoers . . . though he committed no injustice and spoke no deceit" (53:9). And the awe-inspiring climax and promise of the Songs: "Through his suffering my servant shall justify many and bear their iniquities" (53:11).

It is no wonder that these Songs permeate the vision and imagination of the early Christians, enabling them to find in Jesus the fulfillment of God's promises. At last, they exclaim, the just one, the bearer of God's final salvation, has appeared. The striking newness of the vindication of the crucified Messiah brought to light the true "logic" of all God's interactions with Israel. As Paul Hanson writes:

> The advent of the Messiah was viewed by the disciples of Jesus as an astonishing new act of God, and they responded with an enthusiasm born of a fervent sense of God's nearness. Yet the nature of Jesus and the significance of his message and life were worked out by constant reference to ancient Scripture, as the fullness of quotations from the Hebrew Scripture (in its Greek version) in the New Testament indicates.

Although viewed as a fresh chapter in God's saving approach to humans, it was one growing organically out of the long antecedent history recorded in the Torah and the Prophets.[7]

Continuity and Discontinuity

Thus there is both continuity and discontinuity in the relationship between Israel's faith and the New Testament faith in God centered in Jesus Christ. The God of Israel, the God whose gracious initiative summons a people into covenant relationship, the personal God whose love and compassion extend to all, the God whose way can even embrace and transform suffering is most assuredly the God and Father of our Lord Jesus Christ.

Indeed, the faith experience of Israel, witnessed to in its Scriptures, holds in dynamic tension the transcendent holiness of God and God's radical nearness. Torah, Temple, and Sabbath are embodiments of God's nearness. They mediate God's Word and Spirit, yet never, for that, constrain or limit God. These intimations of presence keep alive in Israel the hope for a fullness of presence, in the words of the prophet Jeremiah, for a new covenant in which God's Law will be written on the people's hearts (Jer 31:31-34).

The eyes of Christian faith perceive this fullness in Jesus Christ. He is Torah, Temple, and Sabbath in person. His crucifixion is the burning bush of God's holiness and his resurrection the "I am" of God's ever presence. The new covenant has been established in his crucified and risen body and will not pass away because, by his Ascension, Jesus' humanity has been assumed into God.

Christian faith does not worship a different God than the God who spoke with Abraham and Moses, Isaiah and Jeremiah. In the Christian liturgy we proclaim the revelation to them to be "the Word of the Lord." But in Christ God's eternal Word has become flesh (John 1:14) and God's eternal Spirit has been poured out upon the community of believers (Acts 2:1-4). Thus a new sense of God impregnates Christians' experience. The God whom Christians worship encompasses Jesus, the only begotten Son and the life-giving Spirit. Later generations of Christians will explicitly articulate this faith in the triune God.

The Divine Pedagogy

Few writers in the history of Christianity have had a keener sense of the progressive nature of God's revelation and its reca-pitulation in Christ than the second-century bishop and father of the church, Saint Irenaeus of Lyons. Irenaeus wrote his treatise *Against the Heresies*, to combat the movement known as "Gnosticism." The Gnostics condemned the material universe as the handiwork of a malignant god and attributed salvation to the good God of the Gospel. They thereby rejected the Old Testament as a spurious revelation. Salvation, in the gnostic understanding, was the liberation of the enlightened spirit from its material prison house.

Irenaeus, by contrast, affirmed the unity of the two testaments, celebrating creation and redemption as the loving work of the generous Father who accomplishes this work by employing his "two hands:" the Word and the Spirit. Matter (*plasma*) is part of God's good creation, and God is the *plasmator* who lovingly shapes the human clay and breathes into it the spirit of life.[8]

One crucial consequence of Irenaeus' understanding of the Bible is that God's revelation is progressive, not because of God's unwillingness to share grace and wisdom with creatures, but because humans must slowly develop, with God's grace, the ca-pacity to receive and abide in God's Word and Spirit. Hence God, for Irenaeus, is the patient pedagogue who adapts to human limitations and gradually transforms fragile humanity so that men and women may come to know and praise God's glory.

Central to Irenaeus' theological vision is that God's definitive salvation is realized in the concrete flesh of Jesus. In his life, death, and resurrection Jesus sums up the whole history of Israel and becomes the head of the new humanity that bears God's Spirit. Thus the reality of "recapitulation" (in Greek: *anakephalaiôsis-kephalé*=head) is key to Irenaeus' understanding in the dual sense of "summing up" and placing under the "headship" of Jesus Christ. The Spirit can transform humanity in the flesh because the Spirit is given through the concrete flesh of Jesus. Here Irenaeus, and the Catholic tradition he exemplifies, differs from all Gnostic attempts to escape the flesh into some "pure" spiritual realm. As Douglas Farrow formulates the issue: "The gnostics tried to come to pneumatology directly, bypassing Jesus' history and the cold hard wood of the cross; but it is only *through* Jesus' history that it is possible to discover the truth about the gift of the Spirit."[9]

Irenaeus reverently meditates upon God's *oikonomia*, or plan of salvation, preparing humankind by his Word and Spirit to become a fit dwelling place where God might dwell. Created flesh is not deprecated, but slowly transformed in Christ and rendered apt for the vision of God. In this context of patient pedagogy, then, Irenaeus' famous declaration takes on its full meaning only in the light of the risen Jesus: "For the glory of God is the living human being, and the true life of humanity is the vision of God."[10]

A renewed evangelization can well take Irenaeus as one of its special patrons. In the face of a contemporary Gnosticism that wastefully degrades material creation and often dishonors and abuses the human body, Irenaeus celebrates the good news of matter's native dignity and wondrous redemption. In a consumerist culture characterized too often by the frenetic pursuit of illusory goals, Irenaeus teaches contemplative attunement to God's patient pedagogy in history and in our lives.

Trinitarian Patterns and Formulas

> When the fullness of time had come, God sent his son, born
> of a woman, born under the law, to redeem those who were
> under the law, so that we might receive adoption as sons. And
> because you are sons, God sent the Spirit of his Son into our
> hearts, crying "Abba, Father!" (Gal 4:4-6)

There is not yet a formal doctrine of the Trinity in the New
Testament. Even in a cursory reading, however, one is struck by
the prevalence of trinitarian patterns. Of significant importance
is that these patterns evoke experiential resonances. In the quote
from Galatians given above, Paul is appealing to distinctive experiences shared with the new Christians to whom he is writing:
"God sent the Spirit of his Son into our hearts, crying 'Abba,
Father!'" Clearly delineated are the three: Father, Son, and Spirit.
But they are not abstract terms of reference; they are concrete
names encountered in preaching and invoked in prayer. Indeed,
that the Aramaic word "Abba" is known and prayed by the Greek-
speaking Galatians is remarkable testimony to the newness of
Christian experience as filial relationship to the Father in Christ.

An experiential context is also evident in the beginning of
what is, arguably, the earliest writing of the New Testament: Paul's
First Letter to the Thessalonians. There we read:

> We always give thanks to God for all of you, mentioning you
> constantly in our prayers, remembering, before our God and
> Father, your work of faith and labor of love and steadfast hope
> in our Lord, Jesus Christ. We know, brethren beloved by God,
> that God has chosen you. For our Gospel came to you not by
> word only, but by the power of the Holy Spirit. (1 Thess 1:2-5)

Paul employs the words "thanksgiving" (*eucharistoumen* in
Greek) and "remembering"—words that suggest a liturgical

reference. And the content of this thanksgiving and remembering displays a trinitarian pattern: our God and Father, our Lord Jesus Christ, the power of the Holy Spirit. The articulation of the new presence of God among humans bears a trinitarian character.

One could continue at length to bring forward other instances from the writings of the New Testament—for example, the Last Supper discourses in the Gospel of John—but the basic pattern has been set. Christian experience embraces Father, Son, and Holy Spirit, or, better, is structured and articulated by invocation of and appeal to them.

What I have called "patterns" is reinforced by trinitarian formulas that appear at critical junctures in the New Testament. So, at the conclusion of Paul's Second Letter to the Corinthians, we read his final benediction: "The grace [*charis*] of the Lord Jesus Christ and the love [*agape*] of God and the communion [*koinô- nia*] of the Holy Spirit be with you all" (2 Cor 13:13). And the Gospel of Matthew culminates in the great evangelical mandate: "Go forth and make disciples of all nations, baptizing them in the name of the Father, and of the Son, and of the Holy Spirit" (Matt 28:19).

So, in the New Testament, the "first order" language of prayer and liturgy clearly gives witness to a threefold sense of God's presence: as Father, Son, and Holy Spirit. This "performative" confession of the trinitarian character of the God made known through Jesus Christ does not mean that further questions and issues had been fully faced and resolved. Let me give two examples of what I mean by the "further questions" that needed eventually to be addressed by the Christian community.

I discussed in the last chapter the Christological hymn found in the Letter to the Colossians. Let us consider briefly the hymn found in the Letter to the Philippians (Phil 2:6-11). It confesses Jesus as "being in the form [*morphé*] of God" (Phil 2:6) and marvels that, nonetheless, "he emptied himself" (the well-known "*kenosis*") and took the "form [*morphé*] of a servant" (Phil 2:7). The hymn concludes with the exhortation that "every tongue confess that Jesus Christ is Lord to the glory of God the Father" (Phil 2:11).

Philippians gives striking expression to the preeminence and uniqueness of Christ (as had the hymn in the Letter to the Colossians). It does so by ascribing to Jesus the designation "Lord" (*Kurios*), the Word used in the Greek translation of the Hebrew Scriptures to designate the God of Israel. It then relates the Lord Jesus to God the Father. But it does not specify further what the relation consists in. How are Jesus and the Father related? This is the further crucial question the hymn does not address.

We find a more explicit approach to this issue in another of the Christological hymns embedded in the New Testament: the famous prologue to the Gospel of John. In the very first verse (John 1:1), the Word (*logos*) is declared to be "with God" (*pros ton theon*), and indeed, himself "God" (*theos*). Here the Word is said to be both in relationship to God, and yet himself God. That relationship is further specified at the end of the hymn in the celebrated verse, "And the Word became flesh and dwelt among us [literally, 'pitched his tent in our midst']; and we have seen his glory, glory as that of an only begotten [*monogenous*] from the Father, full of grace and of truth" (John 1:14).

Thus the prologue introduces the theme of the Father-Son relationship so crucial to the entire Gospel of John. It is clear that the gospel posits a fundamentally unique relationship between Jesus and the One he calls "Father." And even though the disciples are to enter into a filial relation with the Father, this is only possible through Jesus who alone is "the way, the truth, and the life," for, as he tells them at the Last Supper, "no one comes to the Father except through me" (John 14:6).

The prologue of John can be said to mark a theological "advance" in that it provides terms that both relate and distinguish

Jesus and the Father. Like the Father, Jesus is God—as Thomas confesses at the gospel's climax (John 20:28); yet Jesus is not the "Father," but the "Son." To use an expression of the philosopher and theologian Bernard Lonergan, one witnesses here the beginning of a "differentiation of consciousness" wherein questions are raised that require a more developed vocabulary to address them.

The Development of Trinitarian Doctrine

In the New Testament we do not yet find a "second order," more technical language for an elaborated doctrine of the Trinity. That achievement was the work of the ensuing three hundred years of reflection and controversy, culminating in the first ecumenical councils of the church: Nicaea (325) and Constantinople I (381). And it was indeed an intellectual and spiritual achievement of the first magnitude, not a mere dispute about words.[11]

The process of development transpired, of course, in the context of Greek language and thought, but the issues dealt with concerned the very nature of Christian faith and salvation. What does salvation consist in and what is the identity of the Savior? The crisis was precipitated by Arius, a priest of Alexandria in Egypt. He forced the issue by asking simply: who is this Jesus (who all Christians acknowledge to be the bearer of salvation)? And he posed the simple alternative: is Jesus God or creature?

It is important to keep in mind that the prime resources for responding to the question of Arius were shared by all Christians, namely, the writings of the New Testament. Arius, as well as his adversaries, were prepared to say: Jesus is Word, Son, and Messiah as taught in the gospels and Epistles. But when faced with the further question—is this Word, this Son, uncreated or created?—the paths diverged. Arius' response was simple. His logic was straightforward: since the Son (as all admit is) "begotten" of the Father, the Son is dependent upon the Father and must ultimately be a creature. There cannot be "begottenness" in the Godhead.

Having affirmed this, Arius was then prepared to pay the Son every compliment: he is the greatest of all creatures, who alone resides "in the bosom of the Father" (John 1:18) and uniquely makes the Father known. Thus the Son can be hymned and praised, but cannot be worshiped, for God alone can be worshiped.

The challenge posed by Arius occupied the bishops gathered at what proved to be the church's first ecumenical council that met in the city of Nicaea in Asia Minor in the year 325. The famous Creed professed by the council, the Nicene Creed, set forth the belief of Christians. In face of Arius' rationalistic assertion, "if begotten, then created," the bishops affirmed the Mystery of the Son: "eternally begotten, but not created"—words we continue to pray today, without adverting to their full significance.

Since all parties employed the terms found in Scripture, the bishops at Nicaea reluctantly introduced a non-Scriptural term in order to give the authentic sense of Scripture: *homoousios*. They taught that the Son was of the *same being* or *same substance* as the Father. In our present translation at Mass we pray: "consubstantial with the Father."

One important consequence of Nicaea's confession is to safeguard the legitimacy of the church's worship of Christ and its liturgical practice of baptizing in the triune Name. A further consequence is to distinguish the Catholic understanding of God from Arius' Greek-influenced sense of God's utter transcendence that does not permit God's proximity to created reality. Hence, for Arius and his followers, Christ mediates between a distant God and material creation.

The God of orthodox faith is indeed transcendent, but a transcendence that does not exclude saving intimacy to creatures. One of the crucial issues underlying the deliberations of the council is the question of salvation. Is humankind touched directly by God or do we have access to God only though an intermediary, who, though in some sense "divine," is inferior to the one true God, as the Arians held? By contrast, the theo-logic of those who professed the Nicene Creed is that salvation is "nothing less than a real and living union between God and his creatures." Hence, "if it is Christ who joins us to the Father, then Christ must himself be no less than God, and must be equal to the Father in divinity." In Christ "God himself has descended into our midst."[12]

The God of the Arians is a "unitarian" God in whom there is no "begottenness," no "relatedness," majestic in his solitude. The God professed by Nicaea is trinitarian whose unity is a rich, differentiated harmony of Father, Son, and Holy Spirit. The full affirmation of the equal divinity of the Holy Spirit awaited the further development canonized at the First Council of Constantinople in 381.[13] But Nicaea had set the basic parameters of the orthodox understanding of the God revealed in Jesus Christ. As Robert Wilken writes:

> The Councils of Nicaea and Constantinople ensured that Christianity's distinctive understanding of God would become a permanent and enduring part of Christian tradition. Although Christians were unreservedly and unequivocally monotheistic, and believed, along with Jews, and later with Muslims, that there is one God, they understood that God was not a "solitary God," as one church father put it. This affirmation, that God's inner life was triune, was a great impetus to Christian thinking and to spiritual life, for it affirmed that the deepest reality is communal.[14]

Dogma as Mystagogic

"Arianism," as the position associated with Arius came to be known, is not a "hoary" heresy of bygone days; nor is the orthodox teaching affirmed at Nicaea a semantic dispute about words.

There are those today, who without ever having heard the name "Arius," nonetheless assume positions that resemble those judged inadequate by the early councils of the church. Whatever the good intentions of those who espouse a view of Jesus as "prophet," "sublime teacher," or "superstar," the effect is to reduce him to our measure, rather than allow ourselves to be measured by him. As maintained in the previous chapter, without confessing the fullness of the church's faith regarding Jesus, we have no grounds for confessing the church's distinctive faith regarding the trinitarian nature of God.

Though the word, "dogma," sounds invidious to some, the dogma of the Trinity proclaims the church's unique experience and understanding of the God of Jesus Christ. It represents the discernment by the apostolic tradition of the true sense of the New Testament's witness concerning the character of the Christian God and of the salvation accomplished in Jesus Christ.

Flannery O'Connor once wrote: "Dogma is the guardian of mystery. The doctrines are spiritually significant in ways that we cannot fathom."[15] As is clear from her correspondence, this conviction did not preclude O'Connor from probing the meaning of her faith, from reading voluminously in theology and philosophy. She understood that dogmas and doctrines are mystagogic: they point us in the direction of the inexhaustible Mystery and invite us to ponder more fully that we may have life. They are not roadblocks, but guard rails that direct our journey safely.

In the centuries following the fourth-century councils, theologians continued to contemplate prayerfully and intellectually their trinitarian faith. The works of Gregory of Nyssa and Augustine of Hippo, Thomas Aquinas and Bonaventure continue to nourish the church's *intellectus fidei*: its understanding of the faith it prays and lives. In the twentieth century there has been a remarkable resurgence of trinitarian reflection in Europe and the United States, as well as in Latin America and Australia.[16]

Three areas of reflection merit mention. First, there has been a retrieval of the sense of the God of Christian faith as not one being among others, albeit the highest being. Rather God is, in the language of Thomas Aquinas, *Ipsum esse subsistens*, Be-ing itself: the One who gives existence to all reality. As Aquinas' designation (dependent on the revelation of God's Name in the book of Exodus: "I Am who Am") indicates, it is more fruitful to meditate upon the triune God as "verb" rather than "noun." God is fully alive and active. God's very Be-ing is to be an infinite Act of generating, communicating, and sharing. Reality at its roots is Personal, indeed, Tri-personal, and calls forth the emergence of personhood in created reality.

Second, the theological tradition has long understood "person" in the Trinity in terms of relations. There are not three separate Gods. The orthodox Christian tradition is trinitarian, not tritheistic, though it can be misunderstood by Jews and Muslims in this way. As the Creed confesses: "I believe in *one* God" who is Father, Son, and Holy Spirit. The "Three" of the Godhead are not separate beings, but are constituted by their very relationships of generous giving, truthful expressing, and joyful sharing. So intimate is this interrelationship that the tradition has used the Greek term, "*perichoresis*," to express the coinherence, the mutual indwelling of the Three. Hence, all God's action in creation, redemption, and sanctification is the action of the Trinity. The Father always acts through the Son in the Holy Spirit.

Third, the notion of communion (Greek: *koinônia*) emerges as a key binding concept in theology, joining reflection on the Trinity to reflection on the church and the Eucharist.[17] In his first encyclical Pope Francis writes concerning the faith of the believer:

> We can respond in the singular—"I believe"—only because we are part of a greater fellowship, only because we can also say

"We believe." This openness to the ecclesial "We," reflects the openness of God's own love, which is not only a relationship between the Father and the Son, between an "I" and a "Thou," but is also, in the Spirit, a "We," a communion of persons.[18]

Returning to the church's first order language of prayer and praise, we do well to remember the liturgical pattern of the church's prayer. We pray to the Father, through his Son, Jesus Christ, in the Holy Spirit. Christian prayer participates in the very rhythm of trinitarian life. The pattern of our morning prayer is that we, and all created reality, come forth today from the Father, through the Son, his Word of love, in the Spirit of communion. And the temporal rhythm of our own day returns at day's end to the Father, through the Son, in the Spirit. We come forth from God and return to God, the God who is Father, Son, and Holy Spirit. As Flannery O'Connor wrote: "For me a dogma is only a gateway to contemplation and is an instrument of freedom and not of restriction. It preserves mystery for the human mind."[19]

Trinitarian Humanity

Humankind, made in the image and likeness of God (Gen 1:26), is thus created in the image and likeness of the Trinity. A long tradition of theological reflection speaks of the image of God, which we bear, in terms of the intellect and will that characterize human beings as "rational animals." Without denying this fundamental given of humanity's uniqueness, attention has more recently been placed upon the intersubjective nature of humanity. Focusing upon the claim of Genesis that "God created man in God's own image: male and female God created them" (Gen 1:27), the persuasion has grown that human beings are not merely rational animals, but "dialogical animals." They display their essential nature in interpersonal encounter and communication, with the ultimate hope of enjoying communion.

Though probably without warrant in the Hebrew text, a number of fathers of the church distinguished God's "image" and "likeness" with regard to human beings. They suggest that we bear God's image from the moment of our creation, but that we are called to grow into God's likeness by faithfully responding to God's gracious call. Von Balthasar, taking up this insight of the fathers, distinguishes the "spiritual individual" and the "person" who we become through generous self-gift to God and others.[20] This distinction has the merit of highlighting the theological origin and significance of the notion of "person," and of underscoring the inseparability of theology and spirituality. As I have several times insisted, God's revelation calls the human to transformation: "convert for the kingdom of God is at hand!"

Dante, as we have seen, charts this journey of human transformation until he attains the vision of the Holy Trinity. But this is not a solitary vision—an "alone to the Alone." For the God of Christian faith is not "solitary" but a communion of persons. Thus Dante, by his transformed vision, becomes a participant in the great communion of holy ones, symbolized by the white rose of the *Paradiso*. The two aspects of the final transformation are inseparable: the communion of the Trinity enables and sustains the communion of the blessed.

Part of the genius of Dante is his acute realization that sin is the perversion of humanity's yearning for communion. The swirling downward descent of the *Inferno* displays to Dante the pilgrim the myriad modalities of communion's distortion and refusal: the anticommunion that is, at the same time, a never fulfilled longing. Paolo and Francesca, Ulysses, and Count Ugolino are unforgettable figures of desire turned deadly. And at the very bottom of *Inferno* is the three-headed Satan: the very anti-Trinity of perverted communion. Each head is voraciously consuming a sinner who betrayed a friend: the antisacrament of Eucharist corrupted. Only the purification of *Purgatorio* (like the penitential rite of the liturgy) permits entrance to the realm of true communion, the *Paradiso*, where all is praise and thanksgiving, song and dance.

If humanity is indeed created in the likeness of the Holy Trinity, then we are called to a life of dialogue and communion in which we learn the new language of "we." At our deepest, human beings yearn for truth and love, for communion. This yearning for communion is the fertile soil in which the seeds of the New Evangelization can be planted. The baptismal waters poured in the name of the triune God will allow the young plants to grow to the maturity God so desires. But the New Evangelization must also realistically discern the forces at work in a capitalist society to manipulate desire and glorify the autonomous individual as, above all, a consumer.[21]

Having reflected, then, upon Christ's passion for communion and the Trinity as God's own life in communion in the first two chapters, we turn, in the next chapter, to explicit meditation upon the sacrament of the Eucharist: the sacrament of communion.

Caravaggio's "Supper at Emmaus:" Milan, Brera Gallery

Chapter Three

The Eucharist, Sacrament of Communion

Michelangelo Merisi (1571–1610), known by the name of the town of his birth, "Caravaggio," was one of the greatest painters of the Baroque era. The greatness of his art and the tormented nature of his tragic life continue to attract and fascinate. He combined in his person profound religious fervor with passionate erotic yearnings. He was quick both to give and take offense, with violent altercations the inevitable result.

Caravaggio came of age in late sixteenth-century Milan, still bathed in the Catholic Reformation inaugurated by its recently deceased archbishop, Charles Borromeo. Borromeo was the zealous advocate of the Catholic Reformation initiated by the Council of Trent (finally concluded in 1563). In effect, Trent inspired a "new evangelization" that sought to reform abuses and to promote authentic Christian living. Borromeo was strongly influenced by such evangelists as Philip Neri and Ignatius Loyola, alert like them to enlist the aesthetic in the service of the Gospel.

Borromeo understood the power of the image to engage the affections and to bring the scenes of the Bible vividly to life for all, but especially for the unlettered poor. His aim was, through art, to foster the realization of the truth and beauty of the Gospel. Caravaggio's religious paintings "translated" these Borromean principles into images of surpassing power.[1] Caravaggio often depicted traditional biblical scenes in conjunction with figures garbed like people of his own day, thereby fixing in the viewer's imagination the conviction that the events could transpire today, in a tavern or on a journey.

The stylistic innovation most noteworthy in these religious paintings was what came to be called "tenebrism": deep shadows penetrated by a piercing, otherworldly light. Caravaggio's dramatic admixture of light and darkness sets forth in intense fashion the human plight of fallenness and the offer of redemptive grace. Intriguingly, he sometimes places himself in the scene portrayed, looking on from a distance, engulfed in darkness, but drawn by the light of grace.

This painting of the "Supper at Emmaus" is one of two surviving depictions by Caravaggio of the scene of the risen Jesus at supper with the two disciples encountered "on the way" (see Luke 24:13-35). It dates from 1606, after Caravaggio fled Rome because he had fatally wounded a rival in a duel. Compared to the earlier version (now in London's National Gallery), the Milan version is more spare, simplified to the essentials. The surrounding darkness is pierced by the light emanating from the face of the risen One, extending through his hand, raised in blessing, to bathe the eucharistic table and the faces of the onlookers. The intensity of the gaze of one of the disciples and of the innkeeper draws the eyes of the viewer to contemplate "the glory of God on the face of Christ" (2 Cor 4:6). Like the other disciple on Jesus' right, we lean forward as if to embrace the Lord with a mix of wonder and disbelief.

Caravaggio the painter depicts in singular fashion the ongoing drama of incarnation, devoid of any pious spiritualization that camouflages the weariness and vulnerability of the flesh. Caravaggio the person struggles to hold fast to the hope of redemptive transformation in the face of darkness and affliction. His tenebrism translates into extraordinary imagery a verse of Matthew's gospel: "the people immersed in darkness have seen a great light; upon those who dwell in the land and the shadow of death, a light has arisen" (Matt 4:16).[2]

Prelude: Dante's Culminating Vision

Scholars often speak of the consummation of Dante's journey as his vision of the triune God in which the deepest desires of humanity are transfigured and fulfilled. That is correct, but incomplete. For Dante's culminating vision actually embraces three "revelations." Several times in the thirty-third and final canto of the *Paradiso*, the one hundredth of the entire *Commedia*, Dante confesses that his words fall far short of the ineffable reality he experienced. Here is how he struggles to express the vision of the Trinity that he received:

> In the deep, transparent essence of the lofty Light
> there appeared to me three circles
> having three colors but the same extent,
> and each one seemed reflected by the other
> as rainbow is by rainbow, while the third seemed fire
> equally breathed forth by one and by the other.[3]

Just prior to this vision, Dante had experienced and tried to articulate his realization that the created universe, in all its manifold parts, forms but a single volume. The book of creation is sewn and sustained by God's loving providence. But a third dimension of Dante's integral vision has been less attended to. Yet perhaps it is the most compelling and challenging. Addressing the triune Light of the Godhead, Dante exclaims:

> That circling which, thus conceived,
> appeared in You as light's reflection,
> once my eyes had gazed on it a while, seemed
> within itself and in its very color,
> to be painted with our likeness,
> so that my sight was all absorbed in it.[4]

The third aspect of Dante's vision is the incarnation: the humanity assumed by the Second Person of the Trinity. The reflected light who is the Son bears "our likeness." The humanity of Christ has been embraced into the very trinitarian life of God. It is this stupendous realization that totally absorbs Dante's sight, moving him to wonder and praise before "the Love that moves the sun and the other stars."

He Ascended into Heaven

The feast of the Ascension of Jesus Christ seems sometimes to be an orphan feast, outshone by the festal celebrations of Easter and Pentecost. Yet, as Dante's vision makes clear, it is the fulfillment of the incarnation of Jesus Christ. We are accustomed to think of the incarnation as a punctiliar event, celebrated at Christmas. But it may be salutary to reflect on it as a process: the assumption of humanity by the Word from conception to death and transfigured life.[5] Thus the Word of God experiences the whole range of the human and bears it into the bosom of the Godhead. The Ascension is not postscript but recapitulation: taking up the whole history of Christ into the eternal life of God. No wonder Dante was enraptured with joy.

It is because Christ has ascended into the Godhead, sitting in power and glory "at the right hand of the Father," that he is able to be present in our midst. It sounds paradoxical, so accustomed are we to think of Christ's Ascension in terms of absence. He is no longer physically among us. Sometimes it even appears that Jesus is on "sabbatical," until he "comes again in glory to judge the living and the dead." But my contention is that it is the Ascension which makes possible a new and more intense presence of Christ in the church and in the world. Because Christ's humanity has been taken into the eternal life of God, "he always lives to make intercession for us" (Heb 7:25). It is the risen and ascended

Lord who is the principal celebrant at every Eucharist. Because of his Ascension Christ is not "nowhere," but "now/here."

In a fine article, the liturgical scholar Robert Taft writes: "our liturgy does not celebrate a past event, but a present person." Taft continues, "Not only is [Christ's] saving, self-offering eternal; he *is* his eternal self-offering, and it is in his presence among us that his sacrifice is eternally present to us."[6] Christ's eternal self-offering is enacted in time and space at every Eucharist. That is why, though there are many eucharistic celebrations throughout the world, in all the rich diversity of languages, there is only one Eucharist eternally offered by the ascended Christ to the Father in the Holy Spirit. Taft again: "The mystery that is Christ is the center of Christian life, and it is this mystery and nothing else that the church renews in the liturgy so that we might be drawn into it."[7]

We are "drawn into it" over the course of our lifetimes, as humanity is being drawn into the mystery of Christ over the centuries. Thus, though Jesus Christ is truly present in every celebration of the Eucharist, he is always present as the One who is yet to come, the One to whom the Spirit and the Bride incessantly cry: "Amen. Come, Lord Jesus!" (Rev 22:20). There is a dialectic of presence and absence both in the liturgy and in the life of the church that expands our spirits. As St. Augustine indicates in his stress upon the *totus Christus*, the whole Christ is still "*in via*," still attaining its fullness. The mystery of Christ is not exhausted in his eucharistic presence, but beckons believers on to ever greater transformation, "until we all attain to the unity of the faith and the knowledge of the Son of God, to that perfected person, measured by the stature of the fullness of Christ" (Eph 4:13).

Eucharist: Meal and Sacrifice

Two of the most momentous external changes inspired by the Second Vatican Council's liturgical renewal are the placement "facing the people" (*versus populum*) of the altar on which the Eucharist is celebrated and the use of the vernacular. But these external changes have also affected interior attitudes. Together they have fostered a different perception of the role of the priest celebrant and, even more, of how the Eucharist itself is experienced.

To sketch the matter in overly broad terms: the role of the priest, facing the people, now appears to be less "mediator" than "facilitator," less intercessor, more functionary. At the same time, and more to the purpose here, the Mass understood as sacrifice (accented when the imposing high altar formed the backdrop for the celebration), morphed, rather abruptly, into the Mass considered as a meal (celebrated on what is more manifestly a table—sometimes constructed of not very substantial material). The further commendable practice of receiving the Eucharist both under the species of bread and wine only added to the growing perception of the Eucharist as "the Lord's Supper."

I am far from deprecating the conciliar-governed reforms that have occurred, though their specific implementation has often proved pastorally poor. My purpose, rather, is to offer a corrective to what can be a reductive understanding of the Eucharistic Mystery by a one-sided focus on one or another of its constitutive elements. It is well known that Benedict XVI expressed reservations about the new placement of the altar. Not because he is not committed to "full participation" of the whole assembly in the eucharistic celebration, but because he desires that the participation in question be in the paschal mystery of Christ, which is the heart of the celebration. It is not what we do that is primary, but what God has done and is doing through Jesus Christ.[8] In effect, Benedict advocates what Robert Taft stressed in the quote I already cited: "The mystery that is Christ is the center of Christian life, and it is this mystery and nothing else that the church renews in the liturgy so that we might be drawn into it."

For this reason Benedict, though he celebrated the Eucharist at the papal altar in St. Peter's Basilica *versus populum*, placed a large crucifix upon the altar so that the gaze of both priest and people were upon the Lord. He repeatedly cited St. Augustine's injunction to the congregation: "*conversi ad Dominum*"—"turn to the Lord!" The underlying concern is that the new placement of the altar can breed a "horizontalism" in our spiritual attitude, obscuring the centrality of Christ. The Eucharist is not the self-contemplation and self-celebration of the community, but the community's thankful worship of the Father, through the Son, in the Spirit. As the concluding doxology of the eucharistic prayer exults: "Through Christ, and with Christ, and in Christ, in the unity of the Holy Spirit, all glory and honor is yours, Almighty Father, forever and ever."

The Eucharist is, by its nature, both meal and sacrifice. We truly partake of the Lord's Supper. But it is the *Lord's* supper, the fruit of his sacrifice: the supper of "the Lamb that was slain" (Rev 5:12). The unique meal that is the Eucharist is made possible by the unique sacrifice of Jesus Christ "who, through the eternal Spirit, offered himself without blemish to God" (Heb 9:14). Hence altar and crucifix are inseparable. Jesus Christ's passion for communion, the animating zeal of his earthly life, culminates in his transformation of the cross into the tree of life. He offers himself, then and now, that the new people of God "may have life and have it to the full" (John 10:10). In his profound meditation on the Eucharist, Ghislain Lafont writes:

> The exchange of food joined to the festive confession of faith in Jesus should not be reduced to just any sort of exchange. In fact, very little is present; we have just a little bread and a little wine. But this contains all, for with it we profess the presence of the perfect offering, the body and blood of Christ. What no exchange of food or gifts could realize *is* realized in the

Christian Eucharist: total loss of self for the giving of life and absolute hope for receiving it."[9]

Eucharistic Transformation

The bread and wine offered by the people of God at the celebration of the Eucharist become transformed by the Word and the Spirit into the very body and blood of Jesus Christ. It is the risen, ascended Lord who is truly present as our spiritual food and drink. But he always bears the marks of his personal history, of his crucifixion for our sake.

This transformation of bread and wine has traditionally been designated in Catholic theology with the technical term "transubstantiation." Employing this technical term, we do not thereby gain purchase on the Mystery, but joyfully confess it, before we enter into reverent silence. Like all dogmatic statements (as we saw above), it is mystagogic: a pointing toward the Mystery, without pretense of possessing it. Indeed, we are not possessors of the Eucharist, but possessed by it. Eucharist fulfills and transcends all the intimations inscribed in the human sharing of food: our striving to communicate with the other, our passionate desire for enduring communion. All these human gestures, signified by the bread and wine we offer, are transubstantiated by God's faithful Word in the power of the Holy Spirit into the body and blood of Christ.[10]

It is a common reflection by the fathers of the church that unlike ordinary food, which we consume and convert into our own physical needs, we ourselves are transformed by our reception of Christ's body and blood, becoming incorporated into his body, the church. There is newness here that we must not neglect; indeed, in our "secular age," we must recover and appropriate its startling radicality. As St. Paul urged the Corinthians: "If anyone is in Christ, he or she is a new creation; the old has passed away, behold, the new has come!" (2 Cor 5:17).

One approach to the new that the Eucharist opens may be gleaned from a striking petition in Eucharistic Prayer III. After the consecration, the celebrant continues: "May he make of us an eternal offering to you." The Latin reads: "*Ipse nos tibi perficiat munus aeternum.*" Who is the "he" (*ipse*)? The preceding part of the eucharistic prayer refers to both the Spirit and Christ. So it might be either the Holy Spirit or Christ who makes of us an eternal offering or gift to the Father. My own view is that it is undividedly both. The "two hands of God" (to recall Irenaeus' image) are fashioning us into a gift to God, into Eucharist.

Thus not only are the bread and wine, "fruit of the earth and work of human hands," transformed, we ourselves, the active participants in the eucharistic celebration, pray that we may be transformed! Clearly the question each of us must ask ourselves is: are we serious about our prayer? Do we truly desire transformation into eucharistic selves?

In the liturgy, our prayer for transformation actually begins with the penitential rite as we seek to approach God with hearts purified. But it crosses an important threshold during the exchange that precedes the preface to the eucharistic prayer. To the celebrant's exhortation, "Let us give thanks to the Lord our God," the assembly responds, "It is right and just." Let me urge that our response not be precipitous. We should pause to discern whether we truly desire, in the words of the preface, "always and everywhere to give thanks" to God. Is "making Eucharist" our deepest desire? Do we truly seek to become eucharistic selves—selves who "always and everywhere give thanks to God"? Always . . . everywhere? We should not allow "It is right and just" to slip too easily from our lips without considering what we are really requesting of God for ourselves.

We are called to become a new creation in Christ. The prospect is staggering, indeed cosmic in scope. We need all the strength and support that God's grace can give. Part of that grace is the "cloud of witnesses" (Heb 12:1) with which we are surrounded, the saints of former and new covenants. It is significant that many of the ancient churches were built over the burial places of the martyrs whose eucharistic gift of self inspired their fellow believers "to run with perseverance the course set before us." Nor do we need to have recourse to former times. Our own times are replete with such witnesses to lives transformed in the power of Christ and the Spirit. In their company we too pray for our ongoing transformation. As Lafont writes: "the offerings brought and placed on the altar have to be transformed by the action of the Holy Spirit, just as those who bring them must themselves be transfigured in such a way that in the Spirit there be nothing but an eternal offering."[11]

Eucharistic Consciousness and Practice

The Eucharist has often been called "the medicine of immortality"—it opens the horizon of believers to eternity. But it does so not by fleeing the flesh with its vulnerability and mortality, but by embracing it in Christ. We learn ever so slowly, to share Paul's conviction that "none of us lives to him or herself alone, and none of us dies to self alone. Rather, if we live, we live to the Lord, and, if we die, we die to the Lord. Thus whether we live or we die, we are the Lord's" (Rom 14:7, 8). Eucharist, then, is the potent antidote to excarnation. It does not disdain matter, but transfigures it, revealing and releasing matter's true dignity and calling.

The Greek word *metanoia*, a word that features so prominently in the proclamation of Jesus, is often translated "repentance" or "conversion." It may also be translated, more literally, as "consciousness raising." The ongoing transformation of believers that the Eucharist promotes is the development of a heightened consciousness: an ability to see more attentively, to act more mindfully. The Eucharist fosters the realization that all is gift and that there is nothing we have that "we have not received" (1 Cor 4:7). The Eucharist also teaches us to extend our thanksgiving throughout our day, heedful of the Apostle's appeal: "whatever you do, in word or work, do everything in the name of the Lord Jesus, giving thanks [*eucharistountes*] to God the Father through him" (Col 3:17).

The spiritual traditions and religious families in the church are inspired attempts, in different historical and cultural settings, to embody this consciousness in concrete practices, a concrete rule of life. One of the most fruitful and lasting is found in the Rule of Benedict. Moreover, the Rule has been creatively adapted to nourish the spiritual growth of individuals even in nonmonastic settings, even in a secular age. Indeed, the Rule challenges too facile a separation of "sacred" and "secular." I want to highlight several features of the Rule that can promote what I call a eucharistic consciousness and practice.

A central portion of the Rule is chapter 4, entitled "The Tools for Good Works," or as it is restated at the end of the chapter: "the tools of the spiritual craft" (RB 4.75).[12] Two "tools" of the spiritual craft are particularly important in developing a eucharistic consciousness for all the baptized, whether monks or not. "The love of Christ must come before all else" (RB 4.21) and "Day by day remind yourself that you are going to die" (RB 4.47).

The celebration of the Eucharist, of course, places the love of Christ at the forefront of our lives as Christians. It orders our days and weeks around the Sun who is Christ. In his light we see more clearly ourselves, our commitments, our genuine human loves. In his light we see light.

The disciple of the Lord finds nothing morbid in the injunction to "keep death daily before our eyes." On the contrary, it is both relativizing and liberating. It helps us keep proper perspective upon what we undertake and what we undergo. It frees us from the idolatry that erects penultimate concerns into ultimate concerns. It counters the ego's stratagem of death denial. For "when we eat this Bread and drink this Cup, we proclaim your death, O Lord, until you come again."

Eucharistic consciousness gives rise to eucharistic practice. I highlight two practices endorsed by the Rule that are germane to every form of Christian life. The first is one of the most celebrated elements of the Benedictine tradition: the hospitality shown to guests—a practice that has perdured for fifteen hundred years. Chapter 53 of the Rule begins: "All guests who present themselves are to be welcomed as Christ" (RB 53.1). It continues: "By a bow of the head or by a complete prostration of the body, Christ is to be adored because he is indeed welcomed in them" (RB 53.7).

Note two features of this practice that can often be countercultural in our North American context. It is corporeal and communal. The whole self is extended in welcoming the stranger-guest, to the point of putting one's body "on the line." Further, in a context often defined by an isolated individualism—Taylor's "buffered self"—the guest, the other, is welcomed into the community. The leitmotif is *Pax*—peace. In a world often marked and marred by violence, the stranger is not only received by the community, but the community renders itself vulnerable before the other.

The second practice that has always inspired and delighted me is found in the instruction given to the "cellarer," the person who has charge of the monastery's goods—a key office. The Rule admonishes: "He will regard all utensils and goods of the monastery as if they were sacred vessels of the altar, aware that nothing is to be neglected" (RB 31.10, 11).[13] In our consumerist culture, with built-in obsolescence of the goods we covet, this healthy respect for the materiality of creation is a truly liberating practice. Again, "sacred" and "secular" are not separated by an impermeable barrier, but become diaphanous.

Reverence for persons and respect for material things are key ingredients to the Rule of Benedict and to every Christian life centered upon the Eucharist of Jesus Christ. Reverence and respect for both the material and the spiritual characterize the new self being transformed in the image of Christ. Indeed, the wisdom of the Rule recognizes that the material and spiritual cannot be sundered as one grows into maturity in Christ.

A Striking Witness

It is a remarkable fact that three of the greatest spiritual witnesses of the twentieth century were Jewish women: Edith Stein, Simone Weil, and Etty Hillesum. Each was highly gifted and quite different from the others. Yet each lived an intense spiritual quest in a time of demonic fury that engulfed Europe and especially targeted the Jewish people for extinction.

Edith Stein, student of the great philosopher Edmund Husserl, became a Catholic and a cloistered Carmelite nun, taking the name Teresa Benedicta of the Cross. She perished at Auschwitz in 1942 and was canonized a saint of the church by Pope John Paul II in 1998. Her major work after entering the cloister was *The Science of the Cross*, based upon her profound meditation on the works of the sixteenth-century Carmelite mystic, St. John of the Cross, appropriated through her daily eucharistic contemplation. The importance of Stein's person and her writings will continue to grow in the twenty-first century, illuminating for us what eucharistic consciousness and practice signify.[14]

Simone Weil, a brilliant and excruciatingly sensitive Frenchwoman, composed influential works of philosophy. For her, as for the classical philosophers, philosophy was not a part-time occupation, but a way of life.[15] However, her spiritual quest took a decisive turn, when, as she put it, "Christ himself came down and took possession of me."[16] This mystical experience was occasioned and nurtured by her praying of the great eucharistic poem of the seventeenth-century Anglican priest and poet George Herbert. In his poem "Love (III)," Herbert prays, in dialogue with the Lord:

> Love bade me welcome: yet my soul drew back,
> > Guiltie of dust and sinne.
> But quick-ey'd Love, observing me grow slack
> > From my first entrance in,
> Drew nearer to me, sweetly questioning,
> > If I lack'd any thing.
>
> A guest, I answer'd, worthy to be here:
> > Love said, You shall be he.
> I the unkinde, ungratefull? Ah my deare,
> > I cannot look on thee.
> Love took my hand, and smiling did reply,
> > Who made the eyes but I?
>
> Truth Lord, but I have marr'd them: let my shame
> > Go where it doth deserve.
> And know you not, sayes Love, who bore the blame?
> > My deare, then I will serve.
> You must sit down, sayes Love, and taste my meat:
> > So I did sit and eat.

Though not accepting baptism, this prayer-poem sustained Simone Weil through the dark days of World War II. She died in England on August 24, 1943, having refused, despite her illness, to eat more than what was allotted her compatriots in Nazi-occupied France, uniting with them in intense spiritual communion.

I now want to dwell at greater length on the striking witness of Etty Hillesum, a young Dutch woman of a cultural and cultured Jewish family who perished at Auschwitz in 1943. Her

"Journals" and "Letters," almost miraculously preserved, are an account of spiritual transformation that deserves to be numbered among the classics of spirituality. They are all the more extraordinary in that they were fired in the crucible of utter evil to which, as she writes, Dante's *Inferno* is "comic opera" by comparison.[17]

Her spiritual maturation owed much to a deeply religious, if unconventional, German Jew, Julius Spier, a student of Jung. The relationship between Etty and S. (as she refers to him in her diaries) was at once spiritual, intellectual, and erotic. In company with him she probed the writings of Tolstoy and Rilke, St. Augustine and the New Testament. What one witnesses in her diaries and letters is the gradual flourishing of her person and the transformation of the eros into agape, with eros (as in Dante) not denied but transfigured.[18] There are four aspects of this transfiguration that I would lift up.

First, she passes from a nonchalant agnosticism regarding God to a passionate devotion to God who becomes the center and anchor of her life. She sums up her journey in these words: "What a strange story it really is, my story: the girl who could not kneel. Or its variation: the girl who learned to pray."[19]

Second, in learning to pray, thanksgiving became more and more the heart of her prayer. Receiving all as gift, her desire was to share that gift, not primarily by words, but by her actions in the hellish conditions of the Dutch transit camp at Westerbork. Less than a month before being sent to Auschwitz, she writes, "You have made me so rich, oh God, please let me share out Your beauty with open hands. My life has become an uninterrupted dialogue with You, oh God, one great dialogue."[20]

Third, there is a stunning honesty in her discernment both of self and of situations. She saw clearly the death-dealing realities she confronted in Amsterdam in the early forties. But she saw at the same time how fear of death could become oppressive and stifle life itself. In a pellucid passage she writes:

> By "coming to terms with life" I mean: the reality of death has become a definite part of my life; my life has, so to speak, been extended by death, by looking death in the eye and accepting it, by accepting destruction as part of life and no longer wasting my energies on fear of death or the refusal to acknowledge its inevitability. It sounds paradoxical: by excluding death from our life we cannot live a full life, and by admitting death into our life we enlarge and enrich it.[21]

I have no idea whether Etty was at all familiar with the Rule of Benedict, but her words could well be commentary on the passage of the Rule cited above.

Yet this realization did not issue in resignation or passivity. Some of the most searing pages ever penned come from her diary entry of August 24, 1943 (the same day Simone Weil died in England). They were written in Westerbork, describing the utter chaos in the camp as men and women and children were herded together to be transported to Auschwitz. Her depiction of the Camp Commandant equals Dante in descriptive power. The Commandant strode along the train "with military precision . . . absolute master over the life and death of Dutch and German Jews here on this remote heath." She goes on, with unerring eye: "On this cruel morning his face is almost iron grey. It is a face that I am quite unable to read. Sometimes it seems to me to be like a long thin scar in which grimness mingles with joylessness and hypocrisy." Then, with penetrating insight: "And there is something else about him, halfway between a dapper hair-dresser's assistant and a stage-door johnny."[22]

Fourth, despite the demonic surroundings in which she had been plunged, she nevertheless found the strength—the grace—to affirm:

> And yet I don't think life is meaningless. And God is not accountable to us for the senseless harm we cause one another.

We are accountable to Him! I have already died a thousand deaths in a thousand concentration camps. I know about everything and am no longer appalled by the latest reports. In one way or another I know it all. And yet I find life beautiful and meaningful. From minute to minute.[23]

In a striking witness to the depths of eucharistic consciousness and practice at which she arrived, she exclaims: "I have broken my body like bread and shared it out among men. And why not, they were hungry and had gone without for so long."[24] Etty Hillesum is a remarkable witness to the costly freedom, the impossible possibility: "always and everywhere to give thanks."

Semina Eucharistiae

The second-century father of the church, Justin Martyr, spoke of the "*semina Verbi*," the seeds of the Word present in every authentic search for truth. Justin thus acknowledged that the texts of the Greek philosophers formed part of the patrimony of Christians in so far as they contain elements of truth that find their fulfillment in Jesus Christ. More recently, theologians have employed the notion to endorse the dialogue among Christianity and the world religions.

Taking inspiration from this tradition, I suggest that another fruitful line of reflection is to consider "*semina Eucharistiae*," seeds of the Eucharist. Of the three great spiritual figures we discussed in the previous section, only Teresa Benedicta of the Cross participated in the sacrament of the Eucharist daily since her conversion to Catholicism. Simone Weil prayed in churches where the Eucharist was reserved, both in Europe and during her brief stay in the United States. To my knowledge, there is no record of Etty Hillesum having direct contact with the sacrament of the Eucharist, though she had Catholic friends and acquaintances. But my discussion of her writings sought to show how "eucharistic" was her awareness and practice: receiving all as gift and seeking to become gift for others. This thanksgiving and self-gift constitute the "seeds" of which Eucharist is the perfected sacrament.

Some years ago, randomly turning television channels, I happened upon a documentary about a small South American tribe which had preserved their ancestral ways as hunter-gatherers. It showed a hunter, returned from the hunt, preparing to share his bounty with the rest of the tribe. When asked why he shared with the other members, rather than keep all for himself, he replied: "I care for them; I want them to survive." It struck me then, as it strikes me now: genuine seeds of the Eucharist permeate and sustain the human journey. Yet the radical import of these seeds and signs is only fully revealed in the Eucharist of Jesus Christ. As Denys Turner writes, apropos the theology of Thomas Aquinas, "you do not fully understand the *human* meaning of food until you understand its Eucharistic depth: lurking within the quotidian business of meals is a mysterious dimension waiting to be disclosed. The Eucharist discloses it."[25] There are plentiful grains, scattered throughout human history and experience, gathered into the living bread shaped by Christ and fired by the Holy Spirit.

The first part of Ghislain Lafont's book on the Eucharist is a phenomenological study of eating, drinking, and speaking. He sees them, at their deepest, as a yearning for the integral word spoken and the authentic feast celebrated. He holds that this endless longing, age after age since the creation of humanity, is at last recapitulated and transfigured in the unique Eucharist of Jesus Christ. All our partial words and incomplete sharings are pointers towards, prefigurations of, the wedding feast of the Lamb. Lafont writes:

> Unique among all exchanges and all sharing of food, the Eucharist realizes what it signifies: the complete covenant be-

tween God and human beings. In virtue of this covenant given and celebrated, the next step would be continually to reopen a history that realizes all the projects of the human being . . . But such a history will move forward from the Eucharist in such a way that it opens further to new possibilities of realizing the unique covenant. This is the true "Feast of Humanity."[26]

Eucharist and Eschatology

Were one to read only the austere and rigorous prose of the *Summa Theologiae*, St. Thomas Aquinas would appear the least poetic of men. However, when Pope Urban IV mandated that the Feast of Corpus Christi be extended to the universal church, he entrusted to Thomas the task of composing the office for the feast. Thomas not only assembled the psalms, he composed antiphons and hymns for the celebration. Among the best known is the antiphon he created to accompany the *Magnificat*:

> O Sacrum Convivium,
> In quo Christus sumitur,
> Recolitur memoria passionis ejus
> Mens impleta gratia
> Et futurae gloriae nobis pignus datur.

> O Sacred Banquet
> In which Christ is received
> The memory of his passion is renewed
> The mind is filled with grace
> And the pledge of future glory is bestowed.

The affectivity which, by and large, is absent from the *Summa* finds voice in Thomas's biblical commentaries and in his hymns and prayers. These are all as fully theological as his systematic writings.

Thus in *O Sacrum Convivium*, the three temporal modes of the eucharistic mystery are clearly set forth. There is the memory of the once and for all moment of Christ's sacrifice. There is the joyful realization of present grace. And there is the sure promise the Eucharist provides of consummation in glory. What is perhaps less clearly in evidence here—but is supplied by Thomas's entire eucharistic theology—is that the "present grace" is embodied in the risen and ascended Lord. As Turner says, "For Thomas, then, Eucharistic presence is nothing but the presence of the resurrection itself, more concretely, the presence of the risen Christ himself within time and history."[27] The risen Christ is present as he who comes to recapitulate all things in himself, bringing the story of each and the stories of all to judgment and salvation. He is present as *viaticum*: food for the journey.

A prime motivation of Benedict XVI in advocating the celebration of the Eucharist *ad orientem* was to give greater prominence to its eschatological dimension. The "East" symbolizes the rising Sun and the return of Christ in glory. There is wide agreement that this eschatological dimension needs to be recovered if we are to attain a more comprehensive understanding of the liturgy, and, indeed, of Christian faith. Though chapter 7 of *Lumen Gentium* is entitled, "The Eschatological Nature of the Pilgrim Church and Her Union with the Church in Heaven," it has been sorely neglected in postconciliar theology and preaching. Indeed, in some translations of the documents of Vatican II, the title of the chapter has even been truncated to "The Pilgrim Church."[28]

A small but potentially significant step forward is the more accurate English rendition of the prayer after the "Our Father" at Mass. The Latin reads: "*expectantes beatam spem et adventum Salvatoris nostri Jesu Christi.*" The previous English translation said: "while we wait in joyful hope for the coming of our Savior, Jesus Christ." The present translation prays: "as we await the blessed hope and the coming of our Savior, Jesus Christ." The prayer does not concern how we wait: "in joyful hope;" but the object of our expectation: "the blessed hope"—the eschatological consummation of all in Christ.

The liturgy is eschatologically charged! Our eucharistic celebration of the Lord's Day, the Eighth Day of the new creation, is not the satisfying of an obligation or the enjoyment of a social gathering, but the burning desire to meet the Lord who comes that we and all the world may have life and have it to the full. It is the countering of every tendency in ourselves and our culture toward excarnation, as we embody the Apostle's injunction: "I urge you to offer your bodies as a living sacrifice, holy and pleasing to God, your true worship; not being conformed to this world, but transformed by the renewal of your mind" (Rom 12:1, 2). It is also the burning desire for the consummation of all things: "through Christ and with Christ and in Christ." Father Roch Kereszty puts it well:

> [T]he Eucharist is indeed the best analogy for the world to come, because it is its initial realization. The new universe in which Christ will be "all in all" (Col 3:11) . . . may be conceived of—with Teilhard de Chardin—as the cosmic extension of an unveiled Eucharistic presence. At the current stage of salvation history, the "species" of the consecrated bread and wine point to, but also veil, the presence of Christ. At the end of times, when the whole material universe will be transformed by Christ as an (attenuated) extension of his glorified body, it will no longer hide from us his glory. We will see his presence manifested in the whole cosmos, which will radiate him to all of us.[29]

The New Evangelization will need to accent this eschatological dimension of the Eucharist far more than in the past. It must strive to broaden believers' horizon beyond the one-dimensionality of a secularism that fails to do justice even to the secular. We must learn anew to long ardently for the fulfillment of our ultimate hope: the transfiguration of all in Christ. At the same time, evangelization needs to sharpen believers' vision, cultivating eyes of fire, to perceive the seeds of the Eucharist, the intimations of Christ's real presence, in the everyday lives of Christians and non-Christians alike. For—amending Rahner—the Christian of the future will be a eucharistic mystic . . . or will not be.

The Cross as the Tree of Life: Twelfth Century Mosaic, Basilica of
San Clemente, Rome

Chapter Four

Ecclesia as Call to Holiness

One of the guiding principles of this book is that great works of art can communicate as effectively, and certainly more affectively, than the necessarily abstract renderings of philosophers and theologians. For example, Dostoevsky's *The Brothers Karamzov* is the patient unfolding, through the heights and depths of human relationships, of a single verse from the Gospel of John that serves as epigraph to the novel. "Amen, amen, I say to you: unless a grain of wheat falls into the earth and dies, it remains alone; but if it dies, it bears much fruit" (John 12:24).

In my experience, no work of art depicts this paschal mystery more vividly and movingly than the resplendent twelfth-century mosaic that fills the apse of the Basilica of San Clemente in Rome. It portrays the cross of Christ as the tree of life. The face of the crucified Christ radiates peace. At the foot of the cross stand the Mother of Jesus and the Beloved Disciple, in rapture at the redemption wrought. They are concrete individuals and also symbols of the church that arises from Christ's sacrifice. Perched on the cross, the twelve doves, representing the twelve apostles, ready themselves to fly off in the power of the Holy Spirit to proclaim the Good News to the four corners of the world.

The extraordinary vision of the anonymous artists, however, is yet more catholic. From the cross flow streams of living water, and from them springs a verdant acanthus bush. Its swirling branches enfold and fondle humans in their multiple activities: farming and shepherding, building and studying. Women and men, monks and laborers, even pagan gods are gathered into a holy communion: sacred and secular united in harmony. The crucified and risen Christ reconciles and recapitulates not only humanity, but all of creation.

Splendid as the mosaic is, it but serves as backdrop for the altar upon which the Eucharist is daily celebrated, extending Christ's life-giving sacrifice in space and time. Here art cedes to reality: the bread and wine, fruit of the earth and work of human hands, become the very body and blood of Christ.

It is quite likely that Dante Alighieri paused to contemplate this magnificent mosaic and to participate in the Eucharist at San Clemente during his stay in Rome. The experience may have sustained him on his own transformative journey that gave birth to the Catholic tradition's greatest poem. *The Divine Comedy* is certainly the story of an individual learning how to love truly, purged of self-centeredness and freed to act generously. But it tells a tale that transcends the individual and even history itself. It sings a love song cosmic in scope, because the triune God, revealed in Jesus Christ, is recognized, in the final ecstatic verse of the poem, to be "the Love that moves the sun and the other stars."

Prelude: Dante on Holiness and Reform

A long sequence of cantos of the *Paradiso* relates Dante's stay in the heaven of the sun, the heaven of the theologians. There he encounters two who had a decisive influence upon his own thought: Thomas Aquinas and Bonaventure. They appear especially in cantos eleven and twelve which resemble each other in form and content. In canto eleven Thomas the Dominican sings the praise of Francis of Assisi, the founder of the Franciscan order; while in canto twelve Bonaventure the Franciscan extols Dominic, the founder of the Dominicans. I suggest to my students that we know we are in Paradise when the rivalry of the Orders yields to unstinted praise.

But something else transpires in the two cantos that demands attention. At the end of each one's encomium of the founder of the other's Order, each excoriates the present condition of his own Order. So Thomas decries his fellow Dominicans who "wander off" like a flock forgetful of their true shepherd. Some remain faithful, he admits, "but these are so few that a tiny piece of cloth can furnish all their cowls."[1]

Bonaventure ends his eulogy of Dominic with a stinging denunciation of his own Franciscans. Francis's family, Bonaventure laments, "which started out setting their feet upon his footprints, is now turned backward, setting their toes where once they placed their heels."[2] Backsliding and rancorous disputes threaten the peace and evangelical mission of the Order whose founding held such promise for the reform of the medieval church.

Of course, these sentiments, placed in the mouths of the two saintly theologians, represent Dante's own discernment of the spiritual situation forty years after their deaths. And Dante, no doubt, has his own stake in the matter. But the discernment also embodies a core ecclesial principle: "*ecclesia semper purificanda et reformanda*"—the church ever requires purification and reform. One need only read Paul's First Letter to the Corinthians for ineluctable witness to the fact—just twenty years after the death and resurrection of Jesus!

The fundamental reason for this need is that the church is far more than a worldly institution, even though it always entails some institutional structures and elements. Most fundamentally, it is the bearer in the world of a transcendent treasure: the divine life made possible by Jesus Christ in the power of the Holy Spirit. It bears this treasure "in earthen vessels" (2 Cor 4:7); hence the need for ongoing conversion and reform. But the thrust of the treasure it bears is toward holiness of life. St. Paul insisted in his first letter: "this is God's will—your sanctification" (1 Thess 4:3).

The theme of sanctification permeates the Pauline letters. He writes to the Corinthians: "Do you not know that your body is a temple of the Holy Spirit dwelling within you . . . therefore glorify God in your body!" (1 Cor 6:19, 20). He tells the Romans: "Now that you have been freed from the tyranny of sin, and have become servants of God, the fruit is holiness whose end is eternal life" (Rom 6:22). And Ephesians sets the theme within the eternal plan of God: "who chose us in Christ before the world's foundation that we might be holy and blameless in his sight" (Eph 1:4).

Dante, who audaciously places himself in the rare company of Paul, as one who has been rapt into the heavens, appropriates Paul's prophetic passion. Hence the denunciations of corrupt churchmen and practices that pepper the *Commedia*. They are the inverse of his realization of the radical conversion and newness of life to which the Gospel summons all Christians.[3] The failure of pastors and prelates is the most reprehensible. They feed themselves rather than nourish those committed to their care—and heaven groans.

New Being

The great French theologian Henri de Lubac wrote: "Everything in the church is ordered toward the new creature (2 Cor 5:17); everything is done for the sake of our sanctification which is, at the same time, our being perfected in unity (according to Jesus' own words: John 17:17-23)."[4] It is crucial in our secular age to underscore this "newness" to which we are called and in which we are participants. For it can too easily be dulled by the relentless sameness and superficiality of a consumer society. It is all the more imperative to do so as we embark upon a "new evangelization." Baptism, the sacramental initiation into the church of God, is not the celebration of birth, but of rebirth; not creation, but new creation. Dying with Christ precedes rising to new life in Christ.

In chapter 1 of this work, therefore, we placed emphasis upon "the originality and uniqueness" of Jesus Christ: Jesus as the new Adam, the beginning of God's new creation. In chapter 2 we stressed the new sense of God as triune, following the Christian claim regarding Christ's unique sonship. And in the previous chapter, we meditated upon the bread and wine offered by the liturgical assembly that is transformed by the power of the Word and the Spirit into the very body of Christ. As we reflect upon "church," it is important once again to insist upon this radical newness. For though its visible structure bears resemblance to other human institutions and may be studied from a strictly sociological standpoint, its distinctive being and identity elevates it to a supernatural origin and destiny. Its core reality is literally theo-logical. It is indeed "a people," but most distinctively, "the people *of God*."

One door leading to a deeper appreciation of the new reality that is church is to draw upon de Lubac's historical and theological reflection on the "tri-form body of Christ." De Lubac was one of the key figures in the movement called *la nouvelle théologie* that flourished, especially in France, in the 1940s and 1950s. It promoted *ressourcement*, a "return to the sources," an idea that became a significant font of the renewal achieved at Vatican II.[5]

De Lubac's studies in the fathers and the early medieval theologians showed that they had a much more organic understanding of the intimate and inseparable relation: Christ–Eucharist–church. De Lubac expresses the differentiated unity in these words:

> The Head and the members form one single body. The Bridegroom and the Bride are but "one flesh." There are not two Christs, of which one is personal and the other "mystical." Of course, the Head and the members are not to be confused; and Christians are not the physical (or "Eucharistic") body of Christ. The Bride is not herself the Bridegroom. All the distinctions remain; but there is no discontinuity. Moreover, the church is not just any body: she is *the* body of Christ.[6]

The philosophical discipline which reflects upon the mystery of being is "ontology." In speaking of "new being," my contention is that the Christian tradition, reflecting upon its liturgical and communal experience, has unveiled a new understanding of being or reality.[7] Founded in the Christological hymns of the New Testament, especially the prologue of John and the hymn of Colossians, this distinctive Christian experience gives rise to a "Christological ontology." The glorified humanity of Jesus Christ reveals the depths of reality itself. And salvation, as suggested in chapter 2, is incorporation into the very body of the risen Lord. Thus Colossians' conviction: "in Christ all reality holds together" (Col 1:17). And against all Gnostic pretensions towards excarnation, Colossians insists: "In Christ all the fullness of the Godhead dwells bodily [*sômatikôs*], and you are being fulfilled in him who is the Head" (Col 2:9, 10).

Thanks to de Lubac and others inspired by him, Catholic theology has gained a renewed appreciation of the profound new reality into which baptism and Eucharist incorporate believers. Personally appropriating this new reality can lead to an awareness that may justly be called "mystical." Christian mysticism, in contrast to neo-Platonic or East Asian mysticisms, is rooted in the soil of the sacraments. It is inseparably Christic, communal, sacramental, and social.

In the introduction I quoted Karl Rahner to the effect that "the Christian of the future will be a mystic, someone who has experienced something, or will not be."[8] The experience in question is the Christian's being-in-Christ. Ghislain Lafont, in words that savor of de Lubac, sketches this Christic-eucharistic mysticism:

> Our bodies, our blood, and our names are not simply counted alongside the body, the blood, and the name of Jesus. Rather, ours are referred to his, as parts to the whole, as members to the body, as sons and daughters in the Son. The mystery of

the church, as the body of Christ, is included *within* the mystery of Christ risen in his body. It is the same reality seen from different points of view.[9]

Catholic living and thinking have still to catch up with the mystery into which we are baptized and which we receive as our daily bread.

Being *in Christ*, then, is to be immersed in a field of new, life-bestowing communication and communion. Drawing upon de Lubac, the ecclesiologist Jean-Marie Tillard signals one of the spiritual implications and challenges for those called to live this new reality:

> The Spirit's power of recreation is actualized in the existence of a body which must remain a body and not yield to the temptation of breaking apart by letting the gangrene of discord take hold. A broken body is no longer a genuine body. To be able to withstand this temptation, every baptized person receives, in the grace of the broken bread and the shared cup, the power not only to be *in Christ* the reconciler—but to live *from Christ* the reconciler, as a member through whom communion is actualized in the body. The health of the communion, that is, of the ecclesial body of Christ, demands the evangelical health of every member.[10]

This concern for the unity of the ecclesial body is one of the pervading traits of the New Testament. In John's gospel, Jesus' "mystical prayer" is a prayer for the unity of his followers: "that they may be one as you, Father, are in me and I in you: that they may be one in us" (John 17:21). Paul's mystical vision is that all those baptized into Christ Jesus "have put on Christ." Therefore, at their deepest reality: "there is not Jew or Greek, slave or free, male or female for you are all one [*heis*] in Christ Jesus" (Gal 3:27, 28).

It is significant that the Greek word that Paul uses for "one" is *heis*: in effect, one person. The Epistle to the Ephesians, the great ecclesial epistle, persistently urges Christians to "be eager to hold fast to the unity of the Spirit in the bond of peace: for there is but one body and one Spirit" (Eph 4:3). Moreover, for Ephesians, this unity is both a given and a goal. There is a dynamism in the Christian calling toward full maturity in Christ, "growing into Christ who is the Head" (Eph 4:15), to form with him the one "perfected person" (*andra teleion*; Eph 4:13). And, as the rest of the remarkable fourth chapter of Ephesians makes clear, this growth into Christ is a growth in holiness, "putting on the new self [*ton kainon anthrôpon*], created in God's likeness [*kata ton theon*] in true justice and holiness" (Eph 4:24). Unity and holiness are evangelical imperatives of God's church.

The Ecclesial Vision of Vatican II

In discussions of Vatican II one often hears two themes sounded. The first is that Vatican II was a council whose primary focus was the church. There is, of course, considerable truth in the assertion. One need only point out that two of its four Constitutions were *Lumen Gentium,* "The Dogmatic Constitution on the Church," and *Gaudium et Spes*, "The Pastoral Constitution on the Church in the Modern World." In addition, a third Constitution is devoted to the church's liturgy. Yet, as I already indicated in the preface, from a theological point of view, "The Dogmatic Constitution on Divine Revelation" enjoys a primacy. For from God's revelation the identity, mission, and worship of the church proceed. We will see shortly the reflection of this in *Lumen Gentium* itself.

The second theme often raised regarding Vatican II is that it effected a "Copernican Revolution" in Catholic ecclesiology or understanding of church. Here too there is much to recommend the view. As we saw above, one of the great accomplishments of the *ressourcement* theologians like de Lubac was to recover the rich organic understanding of church found in the New Testament and the fathers. In the period after the Protestant Reformation and the Council of Trent, ecclesiology became more and more constricted to the institutional and juridical aspects of church. The great French ecclesiologist Yves Congar, a theologian who played a major role at Vatican II, said that for centuries the Catholic Church had a "hierarchology" rather than a rich and comprehensive ecclesiology. This overriding emphasis on the hierarchical leadership of the church characterized the first draft of what became the Constitution, *Lumen Gentium.*

Thus Vatican II's "Copernican Revolution" consisted in a fundamental repositioning whereby the extended discussion of the church's hierarchical structure only comes in chapter 3 of the document. This is preceded by the famous chapter 2 dedicated to the "people of God." One needs to make clear, however, that the "people of God" comprises all the baptized: ordained, religious, and lay. Too often, chapters 2 and 3 of *Lumen Gentium* are unhelpfully contrasted in postconciliar disputations, as though chapter 2 concerned the laity and chapter 3 the hierarchy. Chapter 2 treats the whole people of God: their common vocation, dignity, and responsibility. *Lumen Gentium* then goes on to treat the distinct callings of the ordained (chapter 3), the laity (chapter 4), and religious (chapter 6), within this one people.

A further consequence of Vatican II's holistic vision of church is that the institutional element of church, its visible structure, so prominent in pre–Vatican II ecclesiology, is not denied, but repositioned. The institutional dimension of *ecclesia*, though not primary, is intrinsic to being church. Hence careless assertions regarding "the institutional church"—as though this were somehow in contrast with a "noninstitutional church" (presumably composed of some enlightened group)—have no support in

Vatican II's ecclesial vision. In an important statement of Catholic ecclesial doctrine *Lumen Gentium* teaches:

> Christ, the one mediator, constituted his holy church in this world as a community of faith, hope, and love, a visible structure, that he sustains unceasingly and through which he pours out truth and grace to all. However, the society endowed with hierarchical organs and the mystical body of Christ, the visible assembly and the spiritual community, the earthly church and the church enriched with heavenly gifts, must not be considered as two separate things. They form but one complex reality, comprising both a human and a divine element. Therefore, the analogy with the incarnate Word is not inappropriate. For, just as the assumed human nature serves the divine Word and is inseparably united to him, serving as a living instrument of salvation, so, in a not dissimilar way, the social structure of the church serves the Spirit of Christ who gives life to the church, causing the body to grow. (LG 8)

Catholic ecclesiology affirms both the visible and invisible dimensions of church: both the institutional and the charismatic. But the institutional exists for the sake of the charismatic; its purpose is to serve the building up of the body of Christ in the Spirit.

However, the stellar achievement of *Lumen Gentium*, too often not given sufficient regard, is chapter 1, "The Mystery of the Church." For the uniqueness of church is that it is far more than a merely sociological reality. It is grounded in the divine life mediated through Jesus Christ. Here is where one finds an intimate connection between *Dei Verbum* and *Lumen Gentium*. Just as divine revelation is far more than propositions, but is, at its heart, fulfilled in the person of Jesus Christ, so the church is not a self-contained institution, but witnesses to what God has done and is doing in Jesus Christ. Thus the very title, *Lumen Gentium*, the "Light of the Nations," is not a reference to church, but to Jesus Christ. He alone is the Light of the nations; the church's purpose is to reflect that light faithfully. And because the church can also obscure the light of Christ, the whole church, the whole people of God must always be purified and reformed.[11]

It is certainly fitting to speak of Vatican II as an "ecclesiological council;" but that viewpoint needs deepening. For though the council issued no formal document on Christology, all its teaching is Christologically saturated.[12] Thus the deepest *ressourcement* the council engaged in was a re-Sourcement: a return to the unique Source who is Jesus Christ. In this regard too Henri de Lubac was a trailblazer. Chapter 6 of his book, *Méditation sur l'église*, is entitled "The Sacrament of Christ." Its influence upon *Lumen Gentium* is pronounced. He writes: "The church is a mystery—one might just as well say: the church is a sacrament . . . Here below she is the sacrament of Jesus Christ, as Jesus, in his humanity, is for us the sacrament of God."[13] Note how *Lumen Gentium* employs both these terms, mystery and sacrament, in speaking of the church. For the most part these terms were absent from the more institutional and juridical outlook of pre–Vatican II ecclesiology.

In addition, de Lubac places the entire mission and ministry of the church in service of Christ. He continues: "The whole purpose of the church is to show us Christ, to lead us to him, to communicate his grace to us. In sum: the church only exists to bring us into relation with Christ. She alone can do so and never ceases to do so."[14] Bringing us into relation with Christ, whom the "*Gloria*" of the Mass acclaims as "alone the Holy One," is the unique way to realize the sanctification of God's "*ecclesia*," the assembly called to worship the living God.

If chapter 1 of *Lumen Gentium* sets forth the distinctive identity of church, it is intimately conjoined to chapter 5, "The Universal Call to Holiness in the Church." The distinguished church historian John O'Malley goes so far as to call this chapter, "perhaps the most remarkable aspect of *Lumen Gentium.*" His remarks, coming from a historian of the ecumenical councils, are particularly noteworthy:

> *Lumen Gentium* thus set the agenda, leading the way for the call to holiness to become one of the great themes running through the council. The documents of Vatican II are thus religious documents in a way notably different from those of previous councils. Holiness, the council thus said, is what the church is all about. This is an old truth, of course, and in itself is not remarkable. Yet no previous council had ever explicitly asserted this idea and certainly never developed it so repeatedly and at length.[15]

The ongoing reform of the church and its fitness for the New Evangelization must be rooted in a deeper awareness of the implications of this intimate nexus between chapters 1 and 5 of *Lumen Gentium*. Entering into the mystery of the church at a contemplative, mystical depth and thirsting for the transformative holiness to which Christ summons the whole people of God—lay women and men, religious, priests, bishops (the *universal* call to holiness!)—is the royal road to the reform of the church. As Mother Teresa would say: "it begins with me."

We often enough speak of Vatican II and invoke (sometimes heatedly) the "rights" of all the baptized. What needs equal attention are the "responsibilities" that baptismal commitment engenders: foremost among these is the commitment to holiness of life and to sharing that life with others.

Dimensions of Church

St. Paul, who spoke of church as an organic unity, also insisted on the diversity of roles and ministries. To the Corinthians he wrote, "you are the body of Christ, members of it individually" (1 Cor 12:27). He goes on in his letter to differentiate the roles of apostles and prophets, teachers, those with the gift of healing, administrators, and speakers in tongues. His teaching to the Romans echoes what he told the Corinthians: Just as in one body we have many members, and all the members do not serve the same function, so we many are one body in Christ and each of us members of one another. Yet the gifts given to each differ (see Rom 12:4-6).

Hans Urs von Balthasar has reflected on this unity of faith in diversity of gifts and has suggested a typology of spiritual roles within the one church of Christ. He associates each with a New Testament figure. The church is "Petrine" in that it has a sacramental office of governance. It is "Pauline" in that it is evangelical and prophetic. It is "Johnannine" in that it cultivates deep interiority and contemplation. These are ideal types and do not preclude one member having multiple gifts. Ideally, the different charisms are complementary, and when coordinated in the Spirit serve to build up the body of Christ. Realistically, however, the different charisms can enter into competition and even conflict; and members of the church can fall into the attitude Paul strongly deprecates: "the eye cannot say to the hand, I have no need of you" (1 Cor 12:21).

In order to instruct his community in the life-giving principle of unity, Paul shows them the way of *agape*, without which all presumed "gifts" are but the clanging gongs of egoism (1 Cor 13). For his part, Balthasar, keeping with his identification of constitutive dimensions of church with New Testament figures, speaks of the "Marian" dimension as the soil in which all the rest is rooted. The Marian is represented supremely by the Virgin's *fiat*: Mary's active surrender to the will of God. This full faith in the Word of God initiates and sustains the creature's spousal relationship with the Creator. The late John O'Donnell, in his study of

Balthasar, gives a fine resumé of the role of Mary in Balthasar's thought:

> In the Catholic understanding of ecclesiology, the church is not merely an ideal to be realized in some utopian existence. The church already exists as the spotless bride in Mary. At the same time Mary is the model for all Christians to imitate. She is the archetype of one who perfectly responds to mission. She becomes fully a person in saying "yes" to her mission. So too each of us becomes a person by saying, "yes," to the unique mission Christ proposes for us.[16]

This Catholic appreciation of the unique role of Mary is richly set forth in the final chapter of *Lumen Gentium*. It is well known that one of the disputes at Vatican II was whether to have a separate document on Our Lady or to include the council's reflection on Mary within the Dogmatic Constitution on the Church. The majority of the bishops voted for the latter; a decision that makes eminent theological sense, for Mary is, indeed, a member of the church.

But some have read this decision as a "demotion" of the place of Mary. A careful reading of chapter 8 of *Lumen Gentium* should be more than sufficient to dispel such a misconception. The council teaches: "[Mary] is hailed as the supereminent and altogether unique member of the church, the outstanding type and exemplar of faith and charity. Instructed by the Holy Spirit, the Catholic Church honors Mary with filial piety and affection as most beloved mother" (LG 53). Further, as Balthasar implied, in Mary the church has already attained a fullness. Calling on the intercession of Mary and imitating her example, the Christian faithful strive "to conquer sin and to grow in holiness" (LG 65).

We note, therefore, the intrinsic connection among chapters 1, 5, and 8 of *Lumen Gentium*. Of all the members of the church, Mary has lived most intimately and fully the mystery of the church, the sacrament of the paschal mystery of her Son. Thereby she has attained in privileged and preeminent fashion the holiness to which all the baptized are called. Finally, she is the Queen of the heavenly assembly to which the earthly church belongs and to which it aspires.[17]

Speaking above of "Eucharist and Eschatology," I regretted the relative neglect, in postconciliar Catholicism, of chapter 7 of *Lumen Gentium* on "The Eschatological Nature of the Pilgrim Church and its Union with the Heavenly Church." Our sense of church is grievously truncated if we fail to realize that it includes many more members than its visible earthly manifestation. The commonality which binds the living and the dead (or, better, the more fully living) is the communion in holiness, the communion of holy ones, united in Christ who alone is truly holy.

Referring to the ascended Christ, I insisted that he was not "on sabbatical," withdrawn from the daily lives of his disciples. Chapter 7 of *Lumen Gentium* confirms this conviction. "Sitting at the right of the Father, Christ continually acts in the world to lead men and women to the church, and through it to unite them more closely to himself, and by nourishing them with his own body and blood make them partakers of his own life of glory" (LG 48). The chapter further speaks of the saints in heaven as examples and companions in our own quest for holiness: "the attainment of perfect union with Christ in which holiness consists." For they, while fully sharing in our humanity, are "more fully transformed into the image of Christ" (LG 50).

The concept introduced earlier in this study—Christification—can well serve to tie together these reflections on church as call to holiness. It is Jesus Christ who, by his passion, death, and resurrection, has redeemed the world. Christians are called not merely to the imitation of Christ but to participation in his own life, gradually becoming transformed from their old self to the new self, recreated according to the image and likeness of their Savior, who loves them and, in the Eucharist, continues to give himself for them. The New Evangelization is not about a program, but about a Person and about participation in the new life he enables.

For the Life of the World

If the call to holiness, to transformation in Christ, is at the heart of what church is about, then it is clear that this call is not a merely individualist, much less private affair. It is radically personal which, as we have seen, means it is relational and ecclesial. But we need to go still further. For the church is not a self-contained entity. If it is sacrament, it both embodies the reality it signifies and bears witness to it. It is both communion and mission. Its joy is not complete until it is universally shared. As the First Letter of John testifies: "What we have seen and heard we proclaim also to you, so that you might have communion [*koinônia*] with us, and our communion is with the Father and his Son, Jesus Christ. We are writing this so that our joy may be complete" (1 John 1:3, 4). The mission of the church to proclaim the Gospel is catholic, not sectarian—it is meant for all.

At Vatican II the two constitutions, *Lumen Gentium* and *Gaudium et Spes* (the Dogmatic Constitution on the Church and the Pastoral Constitution on the Church in the Modern World), are in many ways complementary. But one should avoid simplistic dichotomies. The "dogmatic" constitution has multiple pastoral implications. We have seen how central the chapter on the "Universal Call to Holiness" is. Moreover, the "pastoral" constitution is replete with "dogmatic" principles and assertions. Since *Gaudium et Spes* is often taken as the magna carta of the church's commitment to and involvement in the world, I think it of first importance to underline and elucidate the distinctive theological basis for that commitment. It is radically Christocentric. *Gaud-*

ium et Spes does not detract from the imperative of evangelization; it summons to a more integral effort and commitment.

Gaudium et Spes is epoch making in many respects. It is the one document issued by the council that had no preconciliar text as its basis. It is uniquely the creation of the assembled bishops and their theological advisors. It marks a decided turn from the rather defensive attitude toward the world that characterized the church in Europe since the French Revolution and the onset of modernity. It speaks of the church *in* the modern world and not over against it. It employs by preference terms like "dialogue" and "cooperation;" and admits not only to a desire to communicate, but also to learn. It thus laid the foundation for a renewed commitment to issues of justice and peace in the world that continues to inspire many.

Yet the Constitution by no means neglects the ultimate issue of men and women's eternal salvation. In the face of perennial questions regarding the meaning, dignity, and destiny of human beings, *Gaudium et Spes* builds upon *Dei Verbum* and *Lumen Gentium* to proclaim:

> Christ, who died and rose again for all people, gives to humanity, through his Spirit, light and strength to respond to its supreme calling. Nor is there any other name under heaven given to men and women whereby they might be saved. . . . Therefore, it is in the light of Christ, the image of the invisible God and the firstborn of all creation, that the council intends to address all people to shed light on the mystery of humankind and to cooperate in finding a solution to the outstanding questions of our time. (GS 10)

Consequently, the council undertakes (in a much quoted phrase) "to examine closely the signs of the times [*signa temporum perscrutandi*]"; but it always does so (in a crucial, but less quoted phrase) by "interpreting them in the light of the Gospel [*sub evangelii luce interpretandi*]" (GS 4)—which, of course, means in the light of Christ.

This Christocentric foundation for the church's mission in the world is further explained and developed in section twenty-two of the constitution, a section particularly dear to both John Paul II and Benedict XVI. The council teaches that "only in the mystery of the Word incarnate does the mystery of man and woman find full illumination." For "Christ, the new Adam, in revealing the mystery of the Father's love, fully reveals humankind to itself and makes its supreme calling manifest. So it is in Christ that the truths stated here find both their source and fulfillment" (GS 22).

Echoing the Great Tradition of the undivided church, the council continues: "By suffering for us, Christ not only left us an example to follow, but inaugurated a way wherein life and death are sanctified and receive new meaning." Moreover, this sharing in the paschal mystery of Christ is not restricted to Christians alone. For, "since Christ died for all, and since the ultimate vocation of men and women is truly one, namely, a divine destiny, we must hold that the Holy Spirit gives to each one the possibility of sharing in Christ's paschal mystery, in a manner known only to God" (GS 22). In effect, the council teaches that all grace is paschal and, therefore, Christic.

Sometimes critics of the Constitution charge that it betrays a 1960s-style naïve optimism with regard to the world and its possibilities. However correct such criticism may be concerning some who have appealed to it in only a partial manner, it is not true of the Constitution itself. Here is one assertion among many that disproves the charge. "Holy Scripture and humanity's age-old experience teach us that human progress, which can be a boon, also brings great temptation in its train: the right order of values is disrupted, evil is mixed with good, and both individuals and groups consider only their own advantage and not that of others" (GS 37). If one were to ask how such a state of affairs can be remedied, the council once more has recourse to Christ's paschal mystery. "All human enterprises which are daily put in jeopardy by pride and inordinate self-love, must be purified by Christ's cross and resurrection and thus be brought to fulfillment" (GS 37).

This Christological foundation of *Gaudium et Spes'* vision attains its climax in the last section of "Part One" of the Constitution. Its placement is crucial in that it sums up the first part and prepares the way for "Part Two" that treats "some urgent problems." The section is entitled: "Christ, the alpha and omega." The church's only goal, the council claims, is that the reign of God may come and that the salvation of humankind may be realized. Hence, according to the council, the church is the "universal sacrament of salvation" (*universale salutis sacramentum*; GS 45).[18] And in a hymn of praise to its beloved Lord and Master, *Gaudium et Spes* rejoices: "The Lord is the goal of human history, the point upon whom the desires of human history and civilization converge, the center of the human race, the joy of every heart, the fulfillment of every desire" (GS 45).

Reviewing the Christological richness and depth of the council's teaching in *Gaudium et Spes*, one appreciates that the young Joseph Ratzinger would wholeheartedly welcome its Christ-centered vision. In a well-known commentary on the Constitution, published in 1969, he wrote:

> We are probably justified in saying that here, for the first time in a document of the magisterium, a new type of completely Christocentric theology appears. On the basis of Christ this dares to present theology as anthropology and only becomes radically theological by including man in discourse about God by way of Christ, thus manifesting the deepest unity of theology.[19]

Later, as pope, in his social encyclical, *Caritas in Veritate*, Benedict cites *Gaudium et Spes* six times. He insists that there cannot be love without justice, but that love goes beyond justice, for it is pure gift. And that gift of love is only possible in Jesus Christ who, through his cross and resurrection, has incarnated God's love in the world.

Benedict's successor, in his very first homily to the Cardinals (the day after his election), robustly affirmed this Christocentric vision. Pope Francis told his electors with dramatic rhetoric:

> The same Peter who professed Jesus Christ, now says to him: You are the Christ, the Son of the living God. I will follow you, but let us not speak of the Cross. . . . I will follow you on other terms, but without the Cross.

Francis then retorted vehemently:

> When we journey without the cross, when we build without the cross, when we profess Christ without the cross, we are not disciples of the Lord, we are worldly: we may be bishops, priests, cardinals, popes, but not disciples of the Lord.

Then he underscored the consequence for what it means to be church: "We can journey as much as we want, we can build many things, but if we do not profess Jesus Christ, things go wrong. We may become a charitable NGO, but not the church, the Bride of the Lord."[20] Unless united intimately to Jesus on the one Way he has shown, the Way who he himself is, the church inevitably goes astray.

It comes as no surprise, then, to learn that one of those who has deeply influenced Pope Francis's theological understanding is Henri de Lubac. The *ecclesia Dei*, the church of God, is called to holiness and mission. And that call resounds distinctly from the wood of the cross. In his classic work, *Catholicism*, de Lubac entitled his concluding chapter, *Mysterium Crucis* (the Mystery of the Cross). Without ever denying the integrity of the paschal mystery, of cross and resurrection, he nonetheless affirms: "Humanism is not itself Christian. Christian humanism must be a *converted humanism*. There is no smooth transition from a natural to a supernatural love."[21] Dante would only add: "Amen!"

With regard to the New Evangelization, then, we can paraphrase the pope and declare: "if we proclaim Christ without the cross, we are not proclaiming the Gospel." For the Good News of the cross is that it is not dead wood, but fecund tree of life.

Conclusion

The New Evangelization: Going Forth from the Center

Rediscovering the Christic Center

In the introduction to this book, we explored the work of the philosopher Charles Taylor in order to discern aspects of secularity, the social and cultural milieu in which the Gospel must be proclaimed and heard today. Even if this secular context prevails particularly in Europe and North America, globalization insures that its "social imaginary" impacts far beyond those borders. Indeed, so powerful and influential has the consumerist catechumenate of Western culture become—propelled by advertising and media (both old and new)—that the church's often feeble catechumenate needs to be reoriented and refashioned.[1]

Faced with the challenges and shortcomings a secular imaginary represents, Taylor offers hints of a way forward for believers and the church. He sums them up in a phrase already quoted: "we have to struggle to recover a sense of what the Incarnation can mean."[2] My contention has been that the magisterium of Benedict XVI, especially his homilies, encyclicals, and volumes on Jesus, has been focused on just this endeavor: to recover and expand "a sense of what the Incarnation can mean."

I have attempted, in the four chapters of this book, to offer meditations on a renewed "Christic Center," the living heart of a theology at the service of the New Evangelization. In order to animate, impel, and sustain an evangelical commitment, such a theology must strive to offer a unitary vision. The present book argues that the full meaning of the incarnation only truly appears when seen radiating from its source in the very life of the triune God. The incarnation of Jesus realizes its continuing presence in the sacrament of the Eucharist, and patiently works its ultimate purpose: to fill up the body of Christ—the body of redeemed humanity. These are dimensions of the one enfolding and unfolding mystery: the Love in which we live and move and have our being.

Early in the twentieth century, the poet William Butler Yeats, in his poem *The Second Coming*, lamented: "things fall apart; the center cannot hold." Christians believe that the Center is Christ "in whom all things hold together" (Col 1:17). But that Center must be rediscovered ever anew, in every age and culture. Theology has an important role to play here, clarifying and drawing out the distinctive originality of the Christic Center. However, theology's task, though necessary, is insufficient. The imagination has an indispensable contribution to make. Hence the appeal, in this book, to poets like Dante and painters like Caravaggio. Works of art not only engage the intellect, they touch and stretch the heart's affections. In Cardinal Newman's words, they foster the transition from the "notional" to the "real."[3]

A twenty-first-century American poet bears striking witness to a deeply personal rediscovery of the Christic Center. It is all the more remarkable because his rediscovery of Jesus takes place amidst the excruciating affliction of a rare form of cancer. For Christian Wiman, the paschal mystery is not a merely notional assertion, but a burning experience. In wrestling to express why he is a Christian, he testifies: "Christ's suffering shatters the iron walls around individual human suffering, Christ's compassion makes extreme human compassion—to the point of death even— possible. Human love *can* reach right into death, then, but not if it's *merely* human love."[4]

Coming to grips with Christ's passion affords new insight regarding the resurrection. Wiman muses: "Christ's life is not simply a model for how to live, but the living truth of my own existence. Christ is not alive now because he rose from the dead two thousand years ago. He rose from the dead two thousand years ago because he is alive right now."[5]

Striving to make Christ's paschal mystery one's own is the process I have spoken of as "Christification." Less a possessing Christ than a being possessed by Christ, it is the adventure that forms the very marrow of St. Paul's prayer:

> that I may know Christ and the power of his resurrection, sharing communion [koinônia] with his sufferings, and being conformed to his death that I might attain the resurrection of the dead. Not that I have already received this or attained perfection. But I press on to make it my own, because Jesus Messiah has made me his own. (Phil 3:10-12)

Rekindling the Christic Imagination

This book began when Benedict XVI was Bishop of Rome. As is evident, I have been immeasurably enriched by his Christ-centered preaching and theology. Like countless others, I was awed by his courageous and historic resignation, followed by the election as his successor of one "from the ends of the earth." I had the personal grace of being in Rome for the election of Pope Francis and was moved, with the whole world, by his choice of name and the marvelous gesture of bowing his head to be blessed by the prayers of the people.

In the early months of his pontificate, Pope Francis has proved himself a poet of the common touch—moving many by his simplicity, his warmth, and the clarity of his vision. He is rekindling the Christic imagination for many. Yet whatever the different gifts that Benedict and Francis bring to their exercise of the Petrine ministry, they are at one in their celebration of and commitment to the Christic Center.

I earlier quoted from Francis's first homily to the Cardinals the morning after his election. I want now to quote from the evangelical homily the first Jesuit pope preached to his fellow Jesuits on the Feast of their Founder, Ignatius of Loyola. Reflecting on Ignatius' desire that the company he founded take the name "Jesus" as its central reference and identifying character, Francis asked: "Is Christ the center of my life? Do I really put Christ at the center of my life?" Because there is always the temptation to think we ourselves are the center. And when a Jesuit puts himself and not Christ in the center, he goes astray. And, of course, this question concerns not merely the members of the Society of Jesus. It addresses and challenges all the baptized.

Moreover, as a faithful son of Ignatius, Pope Francis realizes that the Christic Center embraces the church as well—one simply cannot separate the Head from the body. He insists:

> Christ is our life! Further, the centrality of Christ corresponds to the centrality of the Church: they are two focal points that cannot be separated: I cannot follow Christ except *in* the church and *with* the church. And in this case too we Jesuits— and the entire Society—are not at the center, we are, so to speak, "displaced:" we are at the service of Christ and of the church, the Bride of Christ Our Lord, who is our holy Mother the hierarchical church (cf. *Spiritual Exercises*, 353). Men rooted in and founded on the church: this is what Jesus wants us to be. There can be no parallel or isolated path. Yes, ways of research, creative ways, this is indeed important: to move out to the periphery, the many peripheries. For this creativity is vital, but

always in community, in the church. This belonging gives us
the courage to go ahead. Serving Christ is loving this concrete
church, serving her generously and in a spirit of obedience.[6]

Once the Christic Center is firm, we can venture forth to the
peripheries without fear of losing the way.

One sometimes hears the impatient query: "what is this 'New
Evangelization' about which there is so much talk?" A simple an-
swer would be: "look to Rio!" The celebration of World Youth Day
showed evangelization in practice. Of course, World Youth Day is
not an event that can be replicated on a daily basis. But at the heart
of Pope Francis' days in Rio de Janeiro one finds the essence of the
New Evangelization. It is a joyful going forth from the Center to
bring the Good News of Christ to all, especially the most needy.

On his arrival in Rio, Francis echoed Peter in the Acts of the
Apostles, telling Brazil's leaders: "I have neither silver nor gold,
but I bring with me the most precious thing given to me: Jesus
Christ! I have come in his name, to feed the flame of fraternal
love that burns in every heart. I wish my greeting to reach one
and all: *The peace of Christ be with you!*"[7]

Then, at the very first Mass the pope celebrated with the young
pilgrims, he told them:

> I say to every one of you today: "Put on Christ!" in your life,
> and you will find a friend in whom you can always trust; "put
> on Christ" and you will see the wings of hope spreading and
> letting you journey with joy towards the future; "put on Christ"
> and your life will be full of his love; it will be a fruitful life.
> Because we all want to have a fruitful life, one that is life-giving
> for others.

Pope Francis assured them:

> You too, dear young people, can be joyful witnesses of his love,
> courageous witnesses of his Gospel, carrying to this world a

ray of his light. Let yourselves be loved by Christ, he is a friend that will not disappoint.[8]

Then, in the final Mass, before a throng of millions carpeting Copacabana Beach, Pope Francis commissioned them for mission:

> Jesus did not say: "go, if you would like to, if you have the time," but he said: "Go and make disciples of all nations." Sharing the experience of faith, bearing witness to the faith, proclaiming the Gospel: this is a command that the Lord entrusts to the whole church, and that includes you. But it is a command that is born not from a desire for domination, from the desire for power, but from the force of love, from the fact that Jesus first came into our midst and did not give us just a part of himself, but he gave us the whole of himself. He gave his life in order to save us and to show us the love and mercy of God.
>
> Jesus does not treat us as slaves, but as people who are free, as friends, as brothers and sisters. And he not only sends us, he accompanies us, he is always beside us in our mission of love. Where does Jesus send us? There are no borders, no limits: he sends us to everyone. The Gospel is for everyone, not just for some. It is not only for those who seem closer to us, more receptive, more welcoming. It is for everyone.
>
> Do not be afraid to go and to bring Christ into every area of life, to the fringes of society, even to those who seem farthest away, most indifferent. The Lord seeks all, he wants everyone to feel the warmth of his mercy and his love.[9]

In the spirit of Francis, in the spirit of the New Evangelization, we can sum up the thrust of these pages. The church's distinctive mission is its witness and call to the world to find its deepest transformation and true life in Christ for the greater Glory of God—the Glory revealed fully on the Face of Christ Jesus.

Postscript

The Joy of the Gospel

This book was already in first proofs when Pope Francis issued his apostolic exhortation *Evangelii Gaudium*, the Joy of the Gospel.[1] This profound and prophetic reflection will inspire and direct the church's evangelizing mission for years to come. Yet, though I would certainly reference it at a number of points in the course of the foregoing reflections, there is nothing in the book that I would change substantially.[2] Indeed, it confirms the Christocentric substance of these meditations. Thus Francis writes in the opening paragraph of his exhortation: "The joy of the gospel fills the hearts and lives of all who encounter Jesus. Those who accept his offer of salvation are set free from sin, sorrow, inner emptiness and loneliness. With Christ joy is constantly born anew." And it is precisely this joyful encounter that liberates the imagination. To what end? To imagine anew what the incarnation, in all its amplitude, can mean.

In mapping the journey from the Christic center to the peripheries, Francis warns, discerningly, of obstacles on the way. As do Benedict and Taylor, he cautions about the "dark side" of secularity: the individualism it breeds, the relativism it propagates, the consumerism it celebrates, the "throw away" mentality that follows in its wake. Francis draws explicitly on the church's teachings on social justice (already strongly reaffirmed by Benedict XVI in the encyclical *Caritas in Veritate*[3]) to denounce a rapacious economic system that produces the dehumanizing poverty, both material and cultural, of the many.

Pope Francis also bluntly addresses obstacles to the joyful proclamation of the Gospel that reside within the church itself. Among these he lists the lack of a truly collegial sharing of gifts, the insensitivity to new cultural embodiments of the Good News, the clericalism whose motivation is too often power-seeking rather than service of the Gospel. But his discernment presses still deeper.

Francis speaks often of a "worldly spirituality" that has lost its anchor in Christ and the Spirit and drifts aimlessly. Too often we pursue some personal agenda rather than allow Christ and his Gospel to direct and measure all our undertakings. He laments:

> At times our media culture and some intellectual circles convey a marked skepticism with regard to the Church's message, along with a certain cynicism. As a consequence, many pastoral workers, although they pray, develop a sort of inferiority complex which leads them to relativize or conceal their Christian identity and convictions. This produces a vicious circle. They end up being unhappy with who they are and what they do; they do not identify with their mission of evangelization and this weakens their commitment. They end up stifling the joy of mission with a kind of obsession about being like everyone else and possessing what everyone else possesses. Their work of evangelization thus becomes forced, and they devote little energy and very limited time to it. (79)[4]

The only remedy for so radical an alienation is conversion: turning again to the person of Jesus Christ and to the joy of encounter with him. Thus the pope writes: "I invite all Christians, everywhere, at this very moment, to a renewed personal encounter with Jesus Christ, or at least an openness to letting him encounter them. I ask all of you to do this unfailingly each day. No one should think that this invitation is not meant for him or her, since 'no one is excluded from the joy brought by the Lord'" (3).

Francis reiterates here what he has stressed in homilies and talks: the heart of the Gospel is mysticism more than moralism. Of course, Christians must do good and avoid evil. They must come to the aid of the poor and oppressed. They must be concerned about environmental degradation and religious intolerance and persecution. But this moral sensibility flows from a compelling and sustaining vision: the vision of the Lord who was crucified for our justification and raised to life for our salvation. Ultimately, the love of Jesus impels us. So Francis writes:

> The primary reason for evangelizing is the love of Jesus which we have received, the experience of salvation which urges us to ever greater love of him. What kind of love would not feel the need to speak of the beloved, to point him out, to make him known? If we do not feel an intense desire to share this love, we need to pray insistently that he will once more touch our hearts. We need to implore his grace daily, asking him to open our cold hearts and shake up our lukewarm and superficial existence. (264)

And he adds, forthrightly: "A person who is not convinced, enthusiastic, certain and in love will convince nobody" (266).

Francis shares with Benedict XVI and Charles Taylor the firm conviction that the evangelical task is to lead ourselves and others toward a new or renewed encounter with the Mystery of God in Christ. They concur that our communication must be "mystagogical": leading into a deeper realization of the inexhaustible Mystery of our saving God. Such communication values the importance of image and symbol, of art and poetry (as this book has insisted throughout). In short, it requires that evangelizers, homilists, catechists, and theologians have recourse not only to appeals to truth and goodness but to beauty as well. It is worth quoting Francis at length:

> Proclaiming Christ means showing that to believe in and to follow him is not only something right and true, but also something beautiful, capable of filling life with new splendor and profound joy, even in the midst of difficulties. Every expression of true beauty can thus be acknowledged as a path leading to an encounter with the Lord Jesus. This has nothing to do with fostering an aesthetic relativism which would downplay the inseparable bond between truth, goodness and beauty, but rather a renewed esteem for beauty as a means of touching the human heart and enabling the truth and goodness of the Risen Christ to radiate within it. If, as Saint Augustine says, we love only that which is beautiful, the incarnate Son, as the revelation of infinite beauty, is supremely lovable and draws us to himself with bonds of love. So a formation in the *via pulchritudinis* [the way of beauty] ought to be part of our effort to pass on the faith. Each particular Church should encourage the use of the arts in evangelization, building on the treasures of the past but also drawing upon the wide variety of contemporary expressions so as to transmit the faith in a new "language of parables." (167)

The reason evangelizers can venture forth boldly, even to the farthest peripheries, is that their Center is secure: Jesus Christ who is "the same, yesterday, today, and forever" (Heb 13:8). Because he is ever new, he makes all things new.

The theme of the "newness," the "originality," and the "uniqueness," of Jesus Christ has permeated this book. It is at the very heart of the Good News we seek to live and to share. The risen Jesus is the joy of all human desiring. He is, in his very person, the joy of the Gospel. In discussing the "newness of Jesus" in chapter 2 I quoted the splendid exclamation of Saint Irenaeus (so beloved of John Paul II and Benedict XVI). I delight to find that Francis too quotes Irenaeus:

> [A]s Saint Irenaeus writes: "By his coming, Christ brought with him all newness." With this newness he is always able to renew our lives and our communities, and even if the Christian message has known periods of darkness and ecclesial weakness, it will never grow old. Jesus Christ can also break through the dull schemas in which we try to imprison him and he constantly surprises us by his divine creativeness. Each time we return to the source and recover the original freshness of the Gospel, new paths open—creative methods, different forms of expression, more eloquent signs, words filled with renewed meaning for today's world. In reality, every authentic act of evangelization is always "new." (11)[5]

The joy of the Gospel, the joy who is Jesus, enraptures our imagination and transfigures our desire.

"Amen. Come, Lord Jesus!" (Rev 22:20) and renew the face of the earth.

December 8, 2013
Solemnity of the Immaculate Conception of Our Lady

Notes

Preface

1. John Paul II, *Novo Millennio Ineunte*, 57, accessed October 15, 2013, http://www.vatican.va/holy_father/john_paul_ii/apost_letters /2001/documents/hf_jp-ii_apl_20010106_novo-millennio-ineunte _en.html.

2. For a fine presentation of this fuller sense of tradition, see Yves Congar, *The Meaning of Tradition*, trans. A.N. Woodrow (San Francisco: Ignatius Press, 2004).

3. See Joseph A. Komonchak, "Vatican II as an 'Event,'" in *Vatican II: Did Anything Happen?*, ed. David G. Schultenover, (New York: Continuum, 2008), 24–51.

4. A helpful introduction to the crucial issue of the interpretation of the council is Ormond Rush, "Toward a Comprehensive Interpretation of the Council and Its Documents," *Theological Studies* 73, no. 3 (September 2012): 547–69.

5. Translations from the documents of the Second Vatican Council are my own.

6. For reflections on the complementarity of these two crucial ministries within the church, see Robert P. Imbelli, "Theologians and Bishops," in *Theological Education in the Catholic Tradition*, ed. Patrick Carey (New York: Crossroad, 1997), 219–36.

7. In an earlier essay I discussed this at greater length. See Robert P. Imbelli, "The Reaffirmation of the Christic Center," in *Sic et Non: Encountering Dominus Iesus*, ed. Stephen J. Pope and Charles Hefling (Maryknoll, NY: Orbis Books, 2002), 96–106.

8. Pope Benedict XVI, *Jesus of Nazareth: From the Baptism in the Jordan to the Transfiguration*, trans. Adrian J. Walker (New York: Doubleday, 2007), xii.

9. Luke Timothy Johnson, "On Taking the Creed Seriously," in *Handing on the Faith: The Church's Mission and Challenge*, ed. Robert P. Imbelli (New York: Crossroad, 2006), 66, 70.

10. Cardinal Avery Dulles, "The New Evangelization and Theological Renewal," in *Evangelization for the Third Millennium* (Mahwah, NJ: Paulist Press, 2009), 81, 85.

11. In an important study, Khaled Anatolios writes: "the construction of a particular set of interpretations of the primacy of Christ—as applied to the entire Christian narrative but especially as informing the notion of divine transcendence—was central to the development of Trinitarian doctrine." See *Retrieving Nicaea: The Development and Meaning of Trinitarian Doctrine* (Grand Rapids, MI: Baker Academic, 2011), 9.

12. For a helpful treatment see Thomas P. Rausch, *Eschatology, Liturgy, and Christology: Toward Recovering an Eschatological Imagination* (Collegeville, MN: Liturgical Press, 2012).

13. Yves Congar, *The Word and the Spirit*, trans. David Smith (San Francisco: Harper & Row, 1986), 1.

14. I use the term "Christic Center" in this book to evoke the extension of the personal reality of the resurrected and ascended Jesus Christ to embrace his real presence in the Eucharist and his incorporation of believers into his Body, the church. As in the writings of Teilhard de Chardin, it points to the cosmic significance of what is most uniquely personal: Jesus Christ, Alpha and Omega (see Rev 1:17, 18).

15. I have long shared the view pointedly expressed by Cardinal Walter Kasper in his book *Theology and Church* (New York: Crossroad, 1989), 12: "theology is not supposed merely to communicate theoretical, speculative insights. It aims at the actual, specific practice of faith, hope, and love. . . . [Many Christians] cry out at the present time for this spiritual and mystical dimension, which is so inexcusably neglected in the conduct of our average academic theology."

16. John Paul II, *Novo Millennio Ineunte*, 29.

Introduction
Charles Taylor and Pope Benedict XVI: Faith Today

1. Karl Rahner, "Christian Living Formerly and Today," in *Theological Investigations*, vol. 7 (New York: Herder, 1971), 15. For a splendid introduction to the mystical element of Rahner's thought, see Harvey D. Egan, *Karl Rahner: Mystic of Everyday Life* (New York: Crossroad, 1998).

2. Charles Taylor, *A Secular Age* (Cambridge, MA: Harvard University Press, 2007) is indispensable for illuminating the context in which Christian living and theological reflection on the New Evangelization must take place in the North Atlantic world. One discussion of what he means by "the social imaginary" may be found on pages 171–76.

3. There is an interesting parallel in this to the beginning of Joseph Ratzinger's classic *Introduction to Christianity*, trans. J. R. Foster, new ed. (San Francisco: Ignatius Press, 2004). Ratzinger starts with doubt and belief in the world of today.

4. Taylor explicitly invokes the "ressourcement theologians" and their contributions to the council: Taylor, *A Secular Age*, 752, 848.

5. Benedict XVI, *Deus Caritas Est*, 1: translation adjusted from version found at http://www.vatican.va/holy_father/benedict_xvi /encyclicals/documents/hf_ben-xvi_enc_20051225_deus-caritas -est_en.html.

6. Taylor, *A Secular Age*, 730.

7. Ibid., 282.

8. Ibid., 753.

9. T. S. Eliot, "The Dry Salvages," in *Four Quartets* (London: Faber and Faber, 1963).

10. Taylor, *A Secular Age*, 737. Tellingly, Taylor several times employs the term *theosis* (deification)—a term dear to Eastern Christian spirituality.

11. Joseph Ratzinger, *Principles of Catholic Theology: Building Stones for a Fundamental Theology*, trans. Sister Mary Frances McCarthy (San Francisco: Ignatius Press, 1987), 171.

12. Taylor, *A Secular Age*, 751.

13. Joseph Ratzinger, "Christocentrism in Preaching?" in *Dogma and Preaching*, trans. Michael J. Miller and Matthew J. O'Connell from

the 4th German edition (San Francisco: Ignatius Press, 2011), 44. This early essay contains much of the future pope's theology *in nuce* and serves as a splendid introduction to his thought.

14. Benedict XVI, General Audience of 3 October 2012, accessed October 15, 2013, http://www.vatican.va/holy_father/benedict_xvi /audiences/2012/documents/hf_ben-xvi_aud_20121003_en.html.

15. Benedict XVI, "Encyclical Letter *Spe Salvi*: On Christian Hope," 48, accessed October 15, 2013, http://www.vatican.va/holy_father /benedict_xvi/encyclicals/documents/hf_ben-xvi_enc_20071130 _spe-salvi_en.html.

16. Taylor, *A Secular Age*, 732.

17. The American poet Christian Wiman, asks, "do we find the fire of belief fading in us only because the words are sodden with overuse and imprecision, and will not burn?" See *My Bright Abyss: Meditation of a Modern Believer* (New York: Farrar, Straus, and Giroux, 2013), 124.

18. Ratzinger, *Dogma and Preaching*, 57.

19. I have set out the bases and framework for a Christocentric approach to the doing of theology in "The Heart Has Its Reasons: Giving an Account of the Hope That Is in Us," *Origins* 43, no. 7 (June 20, 2013): 103–11.

Chapter One
The Originality and Uniqueness of Jesus the Christ

1. Robert Louis Wilken, *The Spirit of Early Christian Thought: Seeking the Face of God* (New Haven, CT: Yale University Press, 2003), xv.

2. For a discussion of the famous letter of Pliny to Trajan see Frans Jozef van Beeck, *God Encountered: A Catholic Contemporary Systematic Theology*, vol. 1: *Understanding the Christian Faith* (Collegeville, MN: Liturgical Press, 1994), 145–51.

3. The *New American Bible* sets off the three passages in poetic stanzas to indicate their hymnic form. The three so indicated are: John 1:1-5, 10-11, 14; Philippians 2:6-11; Colossians 1:15-20.

4. Translations from the Bible are my own.

5. The term "Christification" is prominent in Orthodox theology as indicating the concrete content of *theosis*: the process of divinization

in Christ. Despite its slightly polemical and not always accurate reading of Catholic theology, one may consult with profit Paul Evdokimov, *Orthodoxy*, trans. Jeremy Hummerstone (Hyde Park, NY: New City Press, 2011), for example: 101, 120, 122, 256.

6. For the crucial significance and importance of the phrase "in Christ" in the Pauline literature, see the somewhat dated (originally written in 1929) but still suggestive work of Albert Schweitzer, *The Mysticism of Paul the Apostle*, trans. William Montgomery (New York: Seabury Press, 1968).

7. Irenaeus of Lyons, *Against the Heresies*, iv, 34, 1.

8. It is suggestive to consider how important prepositions are in the New Testament to express fundamental relationships. Just as Christians are "in" (*en*) Christ, so two other Greek prepositions, *pros* and *hyper*, structure the New Testament's understanding of Jesus Christ himself. He is the one totally related to the Father (*pros*) and totally given for the sake of humanity (*hyper*).

9. See Gerhard Lohfink, *Jesus of Nazareth*, trans. Linda M. Maloney (Collegeville, MN: Liturgical Press, 2012), 257–68.

10. Saint Thomas Aquinas has an important and original treatment of Christ as priest and mediator of redemption. See Jean-Pierre Torrell, "The Priesthood of Christ in the *Summa Theologiae*," in *Christ and Spirituality in St. Thomas Aquinas*, trans. Bernhard Blankenhorn (Washington, DC: Catholic University of America Press, 2011), 126–58.

11. Pierre Teilhard de Chardin, *The Divine Milieu* (New York: Harper & Row, 1960), 46.

12. See von Balthasar's powerful, poetic meditation, *Heart of the World*, trans. Erasmo S. Leiva (San Francisco: Ignatius Press, 1979).

13. This coincidence of Jesus' person and mission has characterized Joseph Ratzinger's reflections on Christology from the beginning of his theological ministry. See especially: *Introduction to Christianity*, trans. J. R. Foster and Michael J. Miller (San Francisco: Ignatius Press, 2004), 196–209.

14. A classic New Testament passage that celebrates this *koinonia*, which is the essence of church, is in the First Letter of John: "We proclaim to you what we have seen and heard, so that you too may have

communion with us: and our communion is with the Father and with his Son, Jesus Christ" (1 John 1:3).

15. Walker Percy, *The Thanatos Syndrome* (New York: Farrar, Straus, and Giroux, 1987); Andre Dubus, "On Charon's Wharf" in *Broken Vessels* (Boston: Godine, 1992), 77–82.

16. One of the finest nontheological treatments of the role that fear of death plays in human behavior, both that of individuals and societies, is Ernest Becker, *The Denial of Death* (New York: The Free Press, 1973).

17. A superb meditation upon the interconnection between fear of "death" and living an illusion is Stanley Hauerwas, with David Burrell, "Self-Deception and Autobiography: Reflections on Speer's *Inside the Third Reich*," in Stanley Hauerwas, *Truthfulness and Tragedy* (Notre Dame, IN: University of Notre Dame Press, 1977), 82–98.

18. William B. Frazier, "The Incredible Christian Capacity for Missing the Christian Point," *America* 167, no. 16 (November 21, 1992): 400.

19. The appearance of F. X. Durrwell's *The Resurrection* (French edition 1950; English translation 1960) marked a milestone in the recovery of the centrality of Christ's resurrection for Catholic theology. For a recent study see, Gerald O'Collins, *Believing in the Resurrection: the Meaning and Promise of the Risen Jesus* (Mahwah, NJ: Paulist Press, 2012).

20. John Henry Newman, "Righteousness Viewed as a Gift and as a Quality," in *Lectures on Justification* (London: Longmans, Green, 1914), 193.

21. Yves Congar, *The Word and the Spirit*, trans. David Smith (San Francisco: Harper & Row, 1986), 6.

22. John Henry Newman, "The Spiritual Presence of Christ in the Soul," in *Parochial and Plain Sermons*, vol. 6 (London: Longmans, Green, 1914).

Chapter Two
"The Love that Moves the Sun and the Other Stars"

1. Henri J. M. Nouwen, *Behold the Beauty of the Lord: Praying with Icons* (Notre Dame, IN: Ave Maria Press, 1987), 17–27. For a superb study of the tradition and the theology of Rublev's masterpiece, see

Gabriel Bunge, *The Rublev Trinity*, trans. Andrew Louth (Crestwood, NY: St. Vladimir's Press, 2007).

2. Dante, *Inferno*, canto 1, lines 1–6.

3. See John Freccero, "The Significance of *Terza Rima*," in *Dante: The Poetics of Conversion*, ed. Rachel Jakoff (Cambridge, MA: Harvard University Press, 1986), 258–71.

4. The unique significance of "covenant" in Israel's experience of God has recently been underlined by Robert Bellah in his monumental work, *Religion in Human Evolution: From the Paleolithic to the Axial Age* (Cambridge, MA: Harvard University Press, 2011), 308–310.

5. Paul Hanson, *The People Called: The Growth of Community in the Bible* (New York: Harper and Row, 1986), 125.

6. The Songs or Oracles of the Servant are Isaiah, 42:1-4; 49:1-7; 50:4-11; 52:13–53:12.

7. Hanson, *The People Called*, 385.

8. A good introduction to the theology of Irenaeus is Douglas Farrow, "St. Irenaeus of Lyons," *Pro Ecclesia* 4, no. 3 (Summer 1995): 333–55.

9. Farrow, "St. Irenaeus of Lyons," 345, n. 43.

10. Irenaeus of Lyons, *Against the Heresies*, IV, 20, 7: "*Gloria Dei vivens homo, et vita hominis visio Dei.*"

11. "It may be that the truly distinctive nature of Christianity's understanding of reality first began to assume concrete conceptual form only in the course of the great doctrinal disputes of the fourth and fifth centuries, when theologians were forced by the exigencies of debate to formulate their beliefs as lucidly and as thoroughly as possible." David Bentley Hart, *Atheist Delusions: The Christian Revolution and Its Fashionable Enemies* (New Haven, CT: Yale University Press, 2009), 203.

12. Ibid., 206.

13. Thus the Creed prayed at the liturgy is properly called the "Nicene-Constantinopolitan Creed."

14. Robert Louis Wilken, *The First Thousand Years: A Global History of Christianity* (New Haven, CT: Yale University Press, 2012), 98.

15. Flannery O'Connor, *The Habit of Being*, ed. Sally Fitzgerald (New York: Farrar, Straus, and Giroux, 1979), 365.

16. For a helpful and accessible overview of trinitarian theology with attention to twentieth-century developments, see Anne Hunt, *Trinity: Nexus of the Mysteries of Christian Faith* (Maryknoll, NY: Orbis, 2005).

17. See John Zizioulas, *Being as Communion: Studies in Personhood and the Church* (Crestwood, NY: St. Vladimir's Press, 1985).

18. Pope Francis, "Encyclical Letter *Lumen Fidei*," (June 29, 2012), 39, accessed October 15, 2013, http://www.vatican.va/holy_father/francesco/encyclicals/documents/papa-francesco_20130629_enciclica-lumen-fidei_en.html.

19. O'Connor, *The Habit of Being*, 92.

20. See Hans Urs von Balthasar, "Theological Persons," part 3, in *Theo-Drama: Theological Dramatic Theory*, vol. 3: *Dramatis Personae: Persons in Christ*, trans. Graham Harrison (San Francisco: Ignatius Press, 1992).

21. For trenchant comments, see Brad S. Gregory, "Manufacturing the Goods Life," chap. 5, in *The Unintended Reformation: How a Religious Revolution Secularized Society* (Cambridge, MA: Harvard University Press, 2012).

Chapter Three
The Eucharist, Sacrament of Communion

1. The literature on Caravaggio is vast and ever growing. For a recent biography that stresses the spiritual influence of Charles Borromeo on Caravaggio's Milan, see Andrew Graham-Dixon, *Caravaggio: A Life Sacred and Profane* (New York: Norton, 2010).

2. The Italian literature on Caravaggio is enormous. A recent insightful study of his paintings is Luca Frigerio, *Caravaggio: La Luce e le Tenebre* (Milano: Ancora, 2010).

3. Dante, *Paradiso*, trans. Robert Hollander and Jean Hollander (New York: Doubleday, 2007), canto, 33, lines 115–20, pp. 825–27.

4. Ibid., 827.

5. The Australian theologian Anthony Kelly writes suggestively: "the bodily resurrection and ascension of Christ inaugurates a new expansion of the incarnation and, consequently, a new way of relating to

Christ." See "The Body of Christ: Amen!: The Expanding Incarnation," *Theological Studies* 71 (2010): 802.

6. Robert F. Taft, "What Is a Christian Feast? A Reflection," *Worship* 83, no. 1 (January 2009): 4 (emphasis mine).

7. Ibid., 11.

8. See his discussion in Joseph Ratzinger, *The Spirit of the Liturgy*, trans. John Saward (San Francisco: Ignatius Press, 2000), 74–84.

9. Ghislain Lafont, *Eucharist: The Meal and the Word*, trans. Jeremy Driscoll (Mahwah, NJ: Paulist Press, 2008), 107.

10. Ibid., 141–58.

11. Ibid., 94.

12. *RB 1980: The Rule of St. Benedict*, ed. Timothy Fry (Collegeville, MN: Liturgical Press, 1981), 187.

13. Ibid., 229 (translation modified). For a fine introduction to St. Benedict, the Rule, and the Benedictine tradition of spirituality, see Esther de Waal, *Seeking God: The Way of St. Benedict* (Collegeville, MN: Liturgical Press, 2001).

14. See, for example, the discussion in Robert Barron's important book, *The Priority of Christ: Toward a Postliberal Catholicism* (Grand Rapids, MI: Brazos, 2007), 281–97; and my review in *Worship* 82, no. 2 (March 2008).

15. See the authoritative treatment of this theme in Pierre Hadot, *Philosophy as a Way of Life: Spiritual Exercises from Socrates to Foucault* (London: Wiley-Blackwell, 1995).

16. Simone Weil, "Spiritual Autobiography," in *Waiting on God*, trans. Emma Craufurd (London: Collins, 1963), 35.

17. Diary entry of "14 July 1942" in Etty Hillesum, *An Interrupted Life: The Diaries of Etty Hillesum—1941–43*, trans. Arno Pomerans (New York: Pantheon, 1984), 155.

18. Just two weeks before his resignation as Bishop of Rome, Pope Benedict made reference to Etty Hillesum in his audience of February 13, 2013—Ash Wednesday. He spoke of her as "a woman transfigured by faith." Accessed October 15, 2013, http://www.vatican.va/holy _father/benedict_xvi/audiences/2013/documents/hf_ben-xvi_aud _20130213_en.html.

19. Diary entry of "10 October 1942" in Hillesum, *An Interrupted Life*, 194.

20. Letter of "18 August 1943" in ibid., 205.

21. Diary entry of "3 July 1942" in ibid., 131, 132.

22. Diary entry of "24 August 1943" in ibid., 217, 218.

23. Diary entry of "29 June 1942" in ibid., 127.

24. Diary entry of "12 October 1942" in ibid., 195.

25. Denys Turner, *Thomas Aquinas: A Portrait* (New Haven, CT: Yale University Press, 2013), 237.

26. Lafont, *Eucharist*, 158.

27. Ibid., 246.

28. Insightful in this regard is the book already referenced: Thomas Rausch*, Eschatology, Liturgy, and Christology: Toward Recovering an Eschatological Imagination.*

29. Roch Kereszty, "Catholicity and the Mission of the Church," *Communio* 39, nos. 1–2 (Spring–Summer 2012): 81. The theme of this important double issue is: "Keeping the World Awake to God: The Challenge of Vatican II."

Chapter Four
Ecclesia as Call to Holiness

1. Dante, *Paradiso*, trans. Robert Hollander and Jean Hollander (New York: Doubleday, 2007), canto 11, lines 131–32.

2. Ibid., canto 12, lines 115–17.

3. To signify this *vita nuova*, Dante coins a word at the beginning of *Paradiso*: *trasumanar* (canto 1, line 70): to go beyond the merely human. It is the equivalent of the mystical tradition's *theosis* or deification.

4. Henri de Lubac, *Méditation sur l'église* (Paris: Aubier, 1953), 124, 125 (my translation). This classic work has been translated into English under the title *The Splendor of the Church*, trans. Michael Mason (San Francisco: Ignatius Press, 1999).

5. For a good introduction to the themes and concerns of the movement and its various participants, see Hans Boersma, *Heavenly Participation: The Weaving of a Sacramental Tapestry* (Grand Rapids, MI: Eerdmans, 2011).

6. De Lubac, *Méditation*, 135 (my translation); *Splendor*, 158.

7. See the densely rich reflections in Aidan Nichols, "A Congruent Ontology," chap. 2 in *Chalice of God: A Systematic Theology in Outline* (Collegeville, MN: Liturgical Press, 2012).

8. Karl Rahner, "Christian Living Formerly and Today," in *Theological Investigations*, vol. 7 (New York: Herder, 1971), 15.

9. Lafont, *Eucharist*, 153.

10. J. M. R. Tillard, *Flesh of the Church, Flesh of Christ: At the Source of the Ecclesiology of Communion*, trans. Madeleine Beaumont (Collegeville MN: Liturgical Press, 2001), 93.

11. Still helpful in discerning the council's achievement and the challenges of its integral reception is Avery Dulles, *The Reshaping of Catholicism: Current Challenges in the Theology of Church* (San Francisco: Harper & Row, 1988).

12. See Robert P. Imbelli, "Do This in Memory of Me: Vatican II Calls to a Renewed Realization of the Primacy of Christ," *America* 208, no. 13 (April 22, 2013): 18–20.

13. De Lubac, *Méditation*, 175; *Splendor*, 202.

14. Ibid., 176; *Splendor*, 203.

15. John W. O'Malley, *What Happened at Vatican II?* (Cambridge, MA: Harvard University Press, 2008), 51.

16. John O'Donnell, *Hans Urs von Balthasar* (Collegeville MN: Liturgical Press, 1992), 119.

17. The first encyclical of Pope Francis, *Lumen Fidei*, concludes with a lovely prayer addressed "to Mary, Mother of the Church and Mother of our Faith," accessed October 15, 2013, http://www.vatican.va/holy _father/francesco/encyclicals/documents/papa-francesco_20130629 _enciclica-lumen-fidei_en.html.

In his apostolic exhortation, *Evangelii Gaudium*, Francis invokes Mary in the concluding prayer as "Bride of the eternal wedding feast" and "Star of the New Evangelization." Accessed December 4, 2013, http://www.vatican.va/holy_father/francesco/apost_exhortations /documents/papa-francesco_esortazione-ap_20131124_evangelii -gaudium_en.html.

18. It is noteworthy that nowhere does the council speak of the church as the "sacrament of the world" (*sacramentum mundi*)—a

designation that became popular after the council and that reflects a more "secularized" notion of the church and its mission.

19. Joseph Ratzinger, "The Dignity of the Human Person," quoted in Larry Chapp, "*Gaudium et Spes* and the Intelligibility of Modern Science," *Communio*, vol. 39, nos. 1–2 (Spring–Summer 2012): 273.

20. Homily of Pope Francis at Mass with the Cardinal Electors, Thursday, March 14, 2013, accessed October 15, 2013, http://www.vatican.va/holy_father/francesco/homilies/2013/documents/papa-francesco_20130314_omelia-cardinali_en.html.

21. Henri de Lubac, *Catholicism: Christ and the Common Destiny of Man*, trans. Lancelot C. Sheppard and Elizabeth Englund (San Francisco: Ignatius Press, 1988), 368.

Conclusion
The New Evangelization: Going Forth from the Center

1. See the essays in Robert P. Imbelli, ed., *Handing on the Faith: The Church's Mission and Challenge* (New York: Crossroad, 2006).

2. Charles Taylor, *A Secular Age* (Cambridge, MA: Harvard University Press, 2007), 753.

3. For an intriguing use of artistic representations of the Trinity to promote such realization, see Sarah Coakley, "Seeing God: Trinitarian Thought through Iconography," chap. 5 in *God, Sexuality, and the Self: An Essay on the Trinity* (New York: Cambridge University Press, 2013).

4. Christian Wiman, *My Bright Abyss* (New York: Farrar, Straus and Giroux, 2013), 155.

5. Ibid., 165.

6. http://www.vatican.va/holy_father/francesco/homilies/2013/documents/papa-francesco_20130731_omelia-sant-ignazio_en.html (translation slightly modified).

7. Apostolic Journey to Rio de Janeiro on the Occasion of the XXVIII World Youth Day, "Welcome Ceremony Address of Pope Francis," accessed October 16, 2013, http://www.vatican.va/holy_father/francesco/speeches/2013/july/documents/papa-francesco_20130722_gmg-cerimonia-benvenuto-rio_en.html.

8. Apostolic Journey to Rio de Janeiro on the Occasion of the XXVIII World Youth Day, "Welcoming Ceremony for the Young People Greeting Pope Francis," accessed October 16, 2013, http://www.vatican.va /holy_father/francesco/speeches/2013/july/documents/papa-francesco _20130725_gmg-giovani-rio_en.html.

9. Apostolic Journey to Rio de Janeiro on the Occasion of the XXVIII World Youth Day, "Holy Mass on the Occasion of the XXVIII World Youth Day, Homily of His Holiness Pope Francis," accessed October 16, 2013, http://www.vatican.va/holy_father/francesco/homilies/2013 /documents/papa-francesco_20130728_celebrazione-xxviii-gmg_en .html.

Postscript
The Joy of the Gospel

1. Accessed December 7, 2013; http://www.vatican.va/holy_father /francesco/apost_exhortations/documents/papa-francesco_esortazione -ap_20131124_evangelii-gaudium_en.html.

2. I would especially include Francis's voice and concerns in the conversation and discernment between Benedict XVI and Charles Taylor in the introduction to the book.

3. Accessed December 7, 2013; http://www.vatican.va/holy_father /benedict_xvi/encyclicals/documents/hf_ben-xvi_enc_20090629 _caritas-in-veritate_en.html.

4. One notes in *Evangelii Gaudium*, as in other of the pope's pronouncements, the influence of de Lubac's *Méditation sur l'église* (explicitly quoted in paragraph 93).

5. Translation modified.

Selected Bibliography

Barron, Robert. *Catholicism: A Journey to the Heart of the Faith*. New York: Image Books, 2011. This book with its accompanying ten part DVD series is attractive and accessible for adult education and undergraduate courses in Catholic studies.

De Lubac, Henri. *The Splendor of the Church*. Translated by Michael Mason. San Francisco: Ignatius Press, 1999. This profound meditation on the mystery of church as sacrament of Christ deeply influenced the vision of Vatican II.

Dulles, Avery. *Evangelization for the Third Millennium*. Mahwah, New Jersey: Paulist, 2009. The last book of the first American theologian to be named cardinal. A good primer for the "New Evangelization."

Hunt, Anne. *Trinity: Nexus of the Mysteries of Christian Faith*. Maryknoll, NY: Orbis, 2005. Draws on classical and contemporary Christian theologians to show how theology of the Trinity is interconnected with Christology, Soteriology, and Ecclesiology, as well as its importance for a Christian theology of religions.

Imbelli, Robert, ed. *Handing on the Faith: The Church's Mission and Challenge*. New York: Crossroad, 2006. Essays by prominent scholars treating the context, content, and challenges to communicating faith today.

Lafont, Ghislain. *Eucharist: The Meal and the Word*. Translated by Jeremy Driscoll, OSB. Mahwah, New Jersey: Paulist, 2008. Places the

Eucharist in the context of the human experience of sharing meals and seeking companionship as their fulfillment and transformation.

Lohfink, Gerhard. *Jesus of Nazareth: What He Wanted, Who He Was.* Translated by Linda M. Maloney. Collegeville, MN: Liturgical Press, 2012. An excellent presentation of the life, death, and resurrection of Jesus by a prominent New Testament scholar.

Nichols, Aidan. *Chalice of God: A Systematic Theology in Outline.* Collegeville, MN: Liturgical Press, 2012. Concise and closely reasoned, enhanced with reproductions of icons. Some background in philosophy and theology needed for best appreciation.

Ratzinger, Joseph. *Introduction to Christianity.* Translated by J. R. Foster and Michael J. Miller. San Francisco: Ignatius Press, 2004. The classic work of the young theologian, given as lectures to German university students in 1967.

Rausch, Thomas. *Eschatology, Liturgy, and Christology: Toward Recovering an Eschatological Imagination.* Collegeville, MN: Liturgical Press, 2012. A fine resume of contemporary discussion with balanced appraisals.

Subject Index